HELP ME TALK TO ANYONE

EIGHT SKILLS YOU NEED TO OVERCOME SOCIAL ANXIETY AND ENHANCE YOUR RELATIONSHIPS

VAUGHN CARTER

FURTHER TOGETHER PUBLISHING

CONTENTS

INTRODUCTION

Many years ago, I was invited to a cocktail party to meet new people and make some friends. Sounds fun, right?! More like, *terrifying*. Back then, I would describe myself as a very shy and introverted person. I honestly would have enjoyed staying home and reading a good book. The complete series of Sherlock Holmes wasn't going to read itself, after all.

I also believed I couldn't communicate well with others on their level because of how nervous and anxious I was around new people and crowds. I remember the many thoughts running through my head:

- *What in the world are we going to talk about?*
- *What if it gets awkward?*
- *What if I put my foot in my mouth, again?*

Having lived with these nagging thoughts for most of my life, I made peace with the fact that I simply didn't have the needed conversation skills. It's hopeless. There's nothing I can do about it. That's *some* attitude I had!

Maybe you're wondering how a person like that would get invited in the first place.

Well, someone invited my older brother, and he wanted to help me break out of my shell. We were noticeably different when it came to talking to new people. He was blessed with *extroversion*, which, to me, felt like a superpower that I thought I would never attain myself.

People socially sought after him, and for good reason. He knew how to break the ice, connect easily with others, and could even entertain a whole crowd! So, naturally, I felt more confident around him. And if he was going, the cocktail party couldn't be all that bad, right?

The next thing I knew, we both got dressed up, and hit the road. For my brother, we were heading toward a good time. But for me, a disaster.

About two hours after we arrived, there I was: In the middle of the room, by myself, looking very awkward with a cocktail in hand and no one to talk to. My brother on the other hand, was busy making friends and living his best life.

What was his secret? I mean, *really*?

What was the difference between us two? More importantly, was that a skill I could master myself?

Was being an effective (and enjoyable) communicator possible for someone like me who was shy and reserved? Was I doomed forever?

Are you shy? Does the thought of talking to others make you anxious?

After that evening, I made it my mission to find ways to become a better conversationalist. It was a long and arduous road to improvement, and worth every bit of effort.

How often have you found yourself in a similar position where you feel it best to avoid these types of social scenarios?

The truth is most of us have a wealth of knowledge and a whole truckload of passion for interesting topics. Perhaps you just struggle to package it in a way that draws others in.

Have your friends or family pointed this out to you? Maybe, like me, they called you the shy one. Or they said on your behalf, "They are just quiet." It's not that you don't have something to say, but it's hard when you struggle to get your thoughts across. You have so much information stored up, but the neural connections in your brain don't want to help you relate it to others. And this might cause some anxiety, which stops you dead in your tracks. Like I said, I've been there.

Imagine yourself being a big part of the conversation. There you are, standing tall and looking confident in a small group of people you respect. You're telling your knockout story and building up to the best part. Everyone's eagerly anticipating what you will say next. As they hang on to every word, you dramatically pause before saying the most important part. As the story goes on, it's eating them up inside! The suspense is causing them to sweat. One lady passes out from all the excitement. A man in the group catches her just before she hits the ground. When she finally comes to, all she asks is, "How did the story end?"

With a smile, you kindly explain, "Well, I wouldn't want to bore you all by telling it again."

"No, please!" they say. "We would love to hear it again! Sarah, don't faint this time."

Poor Sarah.

End scene.

Was that a little over the top? Perhaps. A little dramatic? Maybe. But learning to speak to others is not just about exchanging words. We want to be *engaging* while we do it, to connect.

Imagine feeling excited instead of anxious whenever someone mentions a social or corporate gathering.

Imagine being the person in the room that everyone wants to talk to!

Wow. Feels amazing, right? That's exactly what this book will help you to do.

Thankfully, I've learned how to be an effective conversationalist shortly after I started putting value on myself and what I bring to the table. People have been paying more attention to me because I make sure I have something important and valuable to share. And now you can too!

I've gone through all of the same struggles of communicating that you might be experiencing. Maybe you've read other books to help you with this, but it didn't quite suit you. But this book? I share some of the fundamental secrets I've learned that are important for you to become a great conversationalist. Say goodbye to the shyness and lack of social skills and say hello to new friends and improved relationships. Learn how to master small talk and keep a conversation going. And so much more!

My name is Vaughn, and I'm a teacher, consultant, and the author of the best-selling book, *Help Me, I'm Stuck*, which focuses on improving your mindset.

My passion and drive to help others succeed motivated me to write this book. It's difficult to see others struggle with shyness and social anxiety after going through it myself. It's my earnest desire to support them.

In just eight chapters, I will help you improve your social skills, overcome social anxiety, and become the most sought-after person in the room. Just one question:

Are you ready?

INTENTIONS BEHIND INTERACTIONS

There's nothing that does so much harm as good intentions.

— MILTON FRIEDMAN

H ere is a quote that speaks to the fact that good intentions by themselves are not enough. Have you experienced this before?

I remember, many years ago, when I first started a new job. My muscles ache just thinking of the backbreaking labor involved. Enough of it that, for the first time in my life, I had to visit a chiropractor. But it was more than just the labor. There were also techniques to learn and experience to gain in order to be effective. At this particular company, when you were new, there was a saying that goes something like, "You're only useful from the neck down." So, basically, "Do what I say and keep your thoughts to yourself."

Sounds a little harsh, right? But from the upper management's perspective, they were tired of beginners having all kinds of ideas and making suggestions about how they think a job should go. So they were accustomed to shutting the new guys down early on and didn't treat them with a lot of respect until they knew how to handle the tasks properly. Maybe you've had a similar experience.

Well, one day my senior manager made fun of a supervisor because of how he was doing his job. And, between them, it was acceptable because they respected each other and had a lot of experience. The manager was good-humored and always quick with a joke, and it was customary for him to tease other coworkers playfully. Few would say anything in retaliation because he was well respected for his work. One day, I thought it was a good idea to get in on their joke. That was my mistake.

What happened next? We'll finish the story a little later.

But ask yourself: How many times have you said or done something with a specific intention, and the way the person received the message was not how you intended it?

Kind of like an "Oops! That didn't come out right!" Or you thought, "That was the last thing I wanted to happen." I'm sure we've all been there, and it can put a real damper on a conversation and sometimes cause damage to our relationships.

INTENT VS IMPACT

Behind every conversation or interaction, I've discovered there are two important factors for us to consider: The intention behind the conversation and the impact of it. Although we might have good intentions, the way our words are received might not be positive. Why? Because if, at times, we struggle to communicate our intent clearly, it can become easy for something to get lost in translation while conversing with others. How can we avoid this outcome?

To answer this, we first need to understand the difference between the intention and the impact.

So how can we tell the difference between the two? Let's break it down together.

Key Differences Between Intent and Impact

Before we dive into the differences, let's define these two important words.

- **Intent** can be defined as *the goal or aim a person has before they decide to do something*. The goal might be the impact they want to create or the motivation behind what they are planning to say or do.

- **Impact** can be defined as *the outcome or result of their actions* and is not always the same as what they intended.

In other words, intent is *what the person thought* they were doing, while impact is how *others perceive* what the person did.

Keeping that in mind, let's look at two reasons why they don't always align.

- How we feel or think will determine our intent. The impact will be determined by how another person feels based on our actions. When we do something, we do it with intent based on how we feel. The other person may not be on the same page as us and perceive our intent as something else. This can make them feel a different way than what we thought.
- Our intent is directly linked to our personality—who we are as a person—while *the impact is only linked to what we did*. This is such an important thing to remember when things seem to have gone wrong. When someone is explaining to us that our actions hurt them, this is in no way a reflection of who we are as a person. Unless our intention was to hurt them, we shouldn't take it personally but rather listen to understand the impact our actions had and reflect on it.

Examples of Intent vs Impact

As we think about the information above, we come to realize that the disconnect between intent and impact happens more than we might think. We've probably been faced with a few scenarios but never knew that this was a common phenomenon. Rest assured that it is. Why? Because it happens to everyone. Let's look at some everyday examples to bring it closer to home.

- One of your colleagues, who also became your friend, confides in you regarding a work issue they are experiencing. You start brainstorming and sharing ideas about how they can fix the situation, and they become despondent and cut the conversation short. When you approach them later, after they've calmed down, they explain that you made them feel like they did something wrong. Your intent was to support your friend and try to help them fix the problem, but the impact of your actions made them feel like you were judging them and the way they were handling the issue.
- Your child writes their first exam, but it doesn't go well. Their teacher sends the paper home for you to sign, and you decide to have an honest conversation with them on the importance of focusing on their academics. Your intention was to create awareness and show them that you care about their future, but your child perceived it as disappointment.

- You know your significant other better than anyone else, and you understand their humor. They make a joke on a day when you are a little more sensitive, and it hurts you. You know their intention was not to hurt you, but their light-hearted joke had a negative effect on you. Even though you understand their humor and know they meant no harm, the impact their joke had on you was the complete opposite of what they intended.

- You are the manager at a company and realize that one of the processes followed by your employees isn't as efficient as it could be. In an effort to improve efficiency and foster great company culture, you make changes to the process and share this with the team. The team doesn't take it very well and complains the entire meeting. While the intent was to improve the process and team sentiment with a better system, the change had the opposite impact on the team.

Do any of these scenarios sound familiar to you? Let's dig deeper.

Communicating Openly

While this might seem obvious, it's a lot harder than you think. But how so? Communicating openly is not something that comes naturally for everyone.

Each person has a unique perception of the world, including what they believe someone means when they say something. For instance, if you always use humor to lighten a situation, but someone else in the workplace has never been exposed to it in serious settings, they may perceive you as insensitive, and the impact of your light-hearted joke may not be ideal.

When we don't communicate clearly, it's easy for someone to misinterpret the intent behind it and perceive it as something different, leading to conflict.

Not all conflict is bad though.

But why not?

Engaging in *constructive conflict* can be invaluable in any relationship as it helps you to engage meaningfully and find the best solution to the problem at hand.

One way to communicate openly is to be completely honest during the conversation. Now, let's look at another important element to keep in mind.

PURPOSE OF CONVERSATION

There is always a purpose to every conversation, even if it doesn't seem like it. Think about it. Does anyone (with good sense) start a conversation without having a reason behind it? Some conversations can even serve more than one purpose. Take a look at the following list. Which of these common reasons do you normally engage in conversation? Is it:

- Brainstorming or sharing ideas? (Sometimes, we need other people's ideas and opinions to move a project forward.)
- For recognition or reputation purposes? To give recognition or to receive it? (Admittedly, I enjoy recognition when I do something right.)
- To create a new relationship or enhance an existing one? (We have an innate desire to connect with others, and there is no better way than effective communication.)
- Looking for opportunities? (This can be in a personal or professional capacity. By communicating with someone, it's easy to determine which people we will vibe with the most.)
- Just for fun? (Sometimes, it's important to have a conversation for entertainment purposes only or to fill the time.)
- To understand someone else's perspective on something? (This speaks directly to intent and impact as someone's perception can influence both.)

INTENTIONS

It doesn't matter how many times you try to explain your intentions; it can be difficult to get your point across when your actions have left a terrible impact. How so? Let's take a look at how we can explain our intention without making the situation worse.

Setting the Right Intentions and Explaining Our Intent

Setting the intention of each interaction is very important if we want to get the most out of the conversation. *The intention that you set must center around adding value to the other person and your relationship with them.* (This is a KEY point! Could you tell by how I made the sentence *italicized* and put it in **bold** letters?)

The conversation should always be allowed to flow organically. At the same time, we should not just give it free rein because it could quickly become very exhausting for both parties. The perfect middle ground is to *know your intention and make it clear upfront.* (I did that thing again. Did you catch it?)

An important point to stress here is to make sure that we invite another person to join in on a specific conversation. Let them know upfront what route it is likely to take or what we would like to achieve during the discussion with someone else. Although this might not apply to every conversation (such as a random conversation with someone we just met), making sure that we're on the same page will go a long way to ensure it goes as intended.

How can we do this?

Setting the scene and getting the person's **buy-in** is necessary when having an important or complex conversation. This will make a big difference in how productive it is and how invested the other person will be. Without getting their buy-in, we might end up wasting our time and theirs.

This might sound tricky and like a lot of work, but it's normally done effortlessly. How so? Below are some practical examples of ways we can automatically include it in a conversation. Let's see how it could be done:

- "Hey, Jane. I really need your input on this project that I'm working on. Do you have a few minutes to go over some ideas?"
- "Hello, Richard. I've been going over your proposal and have some questions. Can we set up some time to chat about it?"
- "Hi, Harper. The way this role was advertised doesn't seem to align with the daily responsibilities. Do you have a minute to discuss it?"

Pretty easy, right? Making sure that they know what our intention is and asking whether they are willing to participate in the conversation is beneficial. But why exactly is this important?

Consider the following reasons:

- **The person can choose** to either accept or decline your invitation to the conversation. If they accept, they will be more willing to share their thoughts and/or ideas and be completely present in the conversation. They might also suggest an alternative time or date to have it, which will give both of you some time to prepare.
- **You create an expectation** for the other person, so they know what you plan to discuss or address. This helps them to prepare for the conversation instead of feeling surprised. When a conversation catches us off guard, we are more likely to put our walls up and not fully invest.
- **The person you want to have a conversation with has a good idea of what you would like to talk about**. When the "big picture" is not clear to the other person, it's easy for information to get lost in translation.
- By making the intention clear from the beginning and asking for their buy-in, **you also let them know what you expect from them in the conversation**. They don't have to guess what role they need to play.

When we are just planning on having a casual conversation with no clear goal in mind, there is no need to prepare the other person at all. Why? Because their body language and tone of voice should be a clear indication of whether they want to engage in a casual conversation with us or not.

Where Conversations Might Go Wrong

There are a few things that play a role in conversations, which means that there are a few places where the conversation might go wrong, even with good intentions in place. It's important to explore and understand these factors to ensure that we get the most out of our conversations.

According to the linguist, Deborah Tannen, the following aspects will influence your conversation (Gehrt, 2021):

- Your tone of voice.
- How quickly or slowly you speak.
- Where you choose to pause during the conversation.

Keep those three important things in mind: tone, speed, and pausing. She provided further insight into how we can best steer the conversation to reduce the probability that it could go wrong.

She mentioned that the other person's conversational style is very important. There are two factors you should consider: Do they use direct or indirect communication, and are they okay with you joining in while they are talking?

If someone speaks to us with a direct conversational style and we're indirect, then miscommunication is very likely.

Consider the following:

- Someone with a direct conversational tone prefers to get straight to the point. If asked whether they would like to go out to eat, they would simply respond with a yes or a no.
- Someone with an indirect conversational tone gets to the same outcome but in a roundabout manner. When asked whether they would like to go out to eat, they would respond by asking where you had in mind or what you were feeling. They tend to respond with a question.
- If the person has a direct conversational tone, they might misunderstand the person who is indirect by assuming they're not interested due to the additional questions. Someone with an indirect conversational tone would presume that the person responding directly is not interested in any form of communication.

If the person does not like when someone talks over them, they might conceive them as rude instead of an enthusiastic participant.

If our conversational style is not the same as the other person's, the ideal one to use is something in between ours and theirs. A good middle ground is always possible.

Finally, let's give thought to:

- How cultural differences can influence the way an indirect response is perceived. Each culture has a unique way of responding indirectly, so even if we have an indirect conversational tone, we might still misinterpret someone else's reply if their culture is different. It's important to keep this in mind and not assume they had ill intentions when responding.
- The *message* versus the *meta-message*. What the words mean is known as the message, while the meta-message speaks more about what the message says about the relationship with that person. For example, does it show that one person has more power in the relationship than the other or that they are equal? Or does it help us feel closer in the relationship or push us further apart?

When a conversation ends in conflict, it's not about what was said during the interaction but rather about how someone perceived the message (i.e., the meta-message) and how it affected the relationship at the end of the day.

How Intentions Steer Conversations

Before you even start a specific conversation, you already have an idea how it might go and what you hope to get out of it. Your assumptions about a conversation and how it could transpire will influence your intention more often than not and steer the conversation in a specific direction. For instance, if we go into an interaction with the intention of not upsetting the other person because we know their triggers, and what we're about to bring up is one of them, we will go into it feeling anxious and beat around the bush in an attempt to not upset them. Is this the right thing to do?

If they're having a bad day and feel like you're wasting their time, or they prefer direct communication and you're going about it the long way, the conversation will be doomed from the start.

The intention that you take into the conversation (to either prevent or create something) will steer the interaction and how it's structured. You might end up speaking about something completely unrelated by the end of it because the conversation took a different turn than what you wanted.

We should try to avoid making assumptions from the beginning because the truth is we don't know how the conversation will go until we're in it. All we can do is prepare and hope for the best.

Seeing Good Intentions in Others

Now that we understand that the intent might be different to the impact, we'll be able to manage our relationships a lot better.

What to do:

If someone does something that has a negative impact on how we feel, check in with them to understand what their intent was. We might be surprised to discover that most people have good intentions that don't always play out the way they thought it would. The beauty of this is that we have complete control over our thoughts, feelings, and perceptions of a specific situation.

Instead of sulking over what went wrong and pointing fingers, try to understand their intent. We don't have to sweep it under the rug, but we can tactfully point out their mistakes and highlight the impact their actions had without making them feel even worse. A great way to do this is to acknowledge their intent and explain how their actions made us feel.

Remember: The impact their actions have has nothing to do with who they are as a person. It's all about the intentions.

While the person didn't mean to hurt us, it's still a good idea to discuss the situation with them and make sure they understand the impact their actions had.

What to do:

Don't blame them for the way you're feeling. Whether they meant to hurt you or not, avoid putting any blame on them. Instead, let them know how their actions made you feel. Saying "I felt really hurt when you..." versus "You hurt me when you..." will steer the conversation in a completely different direction and open constructive conflict instead of a possible screaming match.

Once you have told them how you feel, give them the opportunity to explain things from their point of view. This won't negate how it made you feel, as your feelings are still valid, but it will help put things into perspective.

Share ideas on how the situation could have been dealt with to ensure a better outcome. Remember to not focus only on their actions but also on how you respond to certain things.

If, at any point during the conversation, one of you gets too upset or worked up, take a break and pick it up again when you have both had some time to cool down and process things.

Intentions You Must Avoid

We already said that our intentions are directly related to who we are as a person. We should assume most people are good at their core, but even good people can have skewed intentions sometimes. There are a few of these that are best avoided for three very good reasons:

- It can drive people away. If we are intentionally being demeaning or manipulating people, they won't stick around. If they are unable to leave, everyone in the equation will be unhappy. Even though we might feel relief after venting or getting our anger out, the feeling won't last once the person decides to retaliate.

- We teach people how to treat us. When we are sarcastic and mean to others, they will find a way to do the same to us, even without their knowledge. This is especially true when engaging and teaching young minds. They will become like the person who had the biggest impact on them, whether good or bad.
- Sometimes, it leads to very bad things. When we force someone to do something they're not comfortable with, it might lead to something very bad happening. We all make bad judgment calls sometimes, which could have catastrophic implications.

Here are some intentions you should avoid (no matter how tempting it is to do otherwise), as they could lead to very unfulfilling conversations and relationships. Some of these may be obvious, but they are worth mentioning.

We should never have a conversation to:

- Avoid acknowledging the other person's feelings and acting as if they are overreacting. We want to treat everyone like their feelings are valid, regardless of whether we agree with them or not.
- Carry out any form of abuse or try to hurt the other person, physically or emotionally.

- Ignore that there is a problem and force our viewpoint onto others.
- Make any threats or make them feel uncomfortable.
- Manipulate or force someone into doing something they might not be comfortable doing.
- Side-step or avoid conversations where we have personally done wrong and pretend like everything is fine.

Adding Value to Others

We've already discussed the reasons why people engage in conversation, and it should come as no surprise that it adds value not only to our lives but to those we engage with.

Here are some ways we can use conversations to add value to others.

Always Think Before You Speak

When something has really upset us, or we're in a bad mood, or not feeling particularly conversational, then sleep on it. We should not bring up anything that we might have a problem with while we're in this state of mind.

If we are someone who needs to get it on paper before we can sleep, type or write it out and then leave it in the "bottom drawer" until the next day. Why? Because if we still feel the same way the next day, we can send the email or have the conversation. Chances are that we'll either change most of the message or decide not to say anything at all.

Ask Questions

Make sure to ask questions during conversations but respect their boundaries.

Asking the other person questions about themselves during a casual conversation or getting their views on something when it's professional is a sure way to add value to any inter-action. What will this do? The person will feel like we are interested in learning more about them and value their input.

In saying that, it's important to know the boundaries when asking questions. We shouldn't ask someone a super personal question about their childhood in the first five minutes of getting to know them.

If we are unsure whether a question is too personal, reflect on whether you would be okay with anyone asking you that question. However, this should not be the only guide. Some-times, if we are thinking about asking someone a personal question, it may help to ask a mature friend for advice. For the sake of privacy, we may give that friend a hypothetical situation and ask if they think the question is too personal. As we all know, our own judgment can be skewed at times, so it's good to get a mature person's perspective on it.

Be Real

People appreciate those who are real, and we're not just referring to being an actual person here. (Unless your name is Pinocchio, and you are made of wood. If this fits your description, I suggest you get medical help immediately. Or call your local Disney theme park, where you will have guaranteed job security.)

Being real means that we don't sugarcoat our words and try to justify our actions when we've hurt someone. It means that we take responsibility for our actions, acknowledge our shortcomings, and are open to constructive criticism to improve ourselves.

It also means that we admit when we feel nervous about a conversation, and we don't try to talk ourselves up to be someone we're not. Sounds fair, right?

Be Simple, Specific, and Straight

During conversations, try to keep it simple, be specific, and get to the point. People don't always have time for long-winded and complex conversations. We should make sure that we understand what we want to say and say it, and ensure that the information is digestible, to the point, and easy to deliver.

Connect Personally

A great way to add value is to connect to someone on a personal level. How so? When we connect with them and talk about something that resonates and is important to them, they are more likely to engage in the conversation. And once we have connected with them personally, it will be a lot easier to get value from the interaction and the relationship in the long run.

A great way to connect with someone on a personal level is to find something you both have in common. Here is where the tip of being real is also very important. Why? Because we shouldn't pretend to have something in common with them just to connect. It's better to be genuine and try to find a way to bring the commonality into the conversation so that they are more at ease when we get into the real stuff.

Keeping it Positive

Using positive communication is so important because as soon as someone uses *but* or *however*, you already know bad news is coming.

When there is bad news, there isn't much we can do about it. The last thing we should do is change the entire message to feed the other person half-truths just to avoid it. The only thing we can do is change these negative words into positive ones. The message will stay the same but the way the message is delivered and, ultimately, received will be different.

Let's look at an example where the word *but* is changed to *and*:

- Your idea is very creative and well thought through, *but* it doesn't meet the needs that we have.

- Your idea is very creative and well thought through *and* with some additional research and collaboration, we can make sure it's fit for purpose.

You could *feel* the difference as you read that, right? One feels more divisive than the other. These two statements will send the conversation in entirely different directions, and the person receiving the second statement will be more receptive to the additional feedback than the one receiving the first.

Listen When They Speak

Being a good listener goes a long way. Sometimes, people really just want someone to listen to them. Their intention is not necessarily to get a response from the other person or wait for a solution. It helps sometimes to just unburden our mind with the challenges we're facing. (For the men out there, please go on YouTube and search, "It's not about the nail.")

Just listening when someone is speaking is not always enough. It's also important to know how to be an empathetic listener, acknowledging their pain but not trying to relate it back to yourself or providing them with any advice. All we should be doing is making sure they know you heard what they said and acknowledging their feelings when it comes to that specific issue.

Empathetic listening sounds easy, but it may be harder than you might think, and only around 2% of the population are able to do it (Sam, 2016).

The Role of Body Language

Pay special attention to body language. Sometimes, our body language says more than our words ever will.

Knowing a few basics on body language goes a long way to determining whether someone is really interested in the conversation or not and whether something specific is a trigger for them.

The gesture most people know how to read is the crossing of arms. Whether the other person knows it or not, by crossing their arms, they are sending the message that they are not very interested in what we're saying and basically closing their minds to the message that's being communicated.

We shouldn't be discouraged when we see this. All we need to do is get them to change their body language. So, making them do something with one or both hands will require them to uncross their arms. For example, if we're dealing with a client and their arms are crossed, a simple trick is to hand them a cup of coffee. It's a thing. And it works.

IMPACT

Even when we have the best of intentions and follow all the guidelines to set the right ones, there is always a possibility that someone can misunderstand them, or they can get lost in translation. We can't control how others feel or how they perceive our actions. They might just be having a bad day, which impacts the way they give and receive information.

While we have no control over that, we do have control over the intentions we have and what we do to make them clear. If someone gets hurt or offended based on our actions, it's important that we acknowledge how it made them feel and whether that was our intention or not. We should be honest and open with them by acknowledging the fact that our actions made them feel a certain way.

There are a few things we can focus on in situations where our intentions weren't clear and impacted someone negatively. It's important to deal with the situation in a sensitive manner and not blame them for being oversensitive. This situation is never easy, but here are some practical things we can do:

- Don't immediately jump to the defense and try to explain what our intentions were. Listen attentively and actively to what they are saying with the intention to understand the impact your actions had, not necessarily to correct their perception of the situation.
- Allow them to feel that way about the situation and acknowledge their feelings. We might also feel a little ruffled knowing that our actions were taken out of

context, but this moment is not about us. Right now, it's about them and the impact our actions had on them. We can share or deal with our feelings around the matter when the dust settles.

- Remember to apologize for the impact our actions had. Take accountability for what happened and avoid putting the blame on them.

Here are some things to avoid saying:

- Don't say, "I'm sorry if…" because there is no if. Our actions hurt them, which is something they already shared with us.
- Don't say, "I'm sorry, but…" because that implies that we're not really sorry and we want to justify what happened.
- Don't say, "I'm sorry you…" as that puts the blame on them. We should never blame them for feeling a certain way about our actions.
- Make sure that we apologize sincerely and commit to trying harder next time.

After considering all of that. Let's return to the story at the beginning of the chapter. While my supervisor took no offense to the manager who was of equal experience and skill, he immediately took what I said as disrespect and reprimanded me on the spot. I was embarrassed more than anything else. My intentions were to just get in on the fun and share a laugh with them. I forgot I was new and wasn't in a position to make light of the way he did his job. Fair enough. A valuable lesson learned: good intentions don't equal a good outcome.

What can further help you avoid a bad outcome?

I've included an intentions worksheet on the next page for initiating conversations. You definitely won't need to physically complete this for every conversation, but it will help to set out everything that you will need to consider.

INTENTION SETTING WORKSHEET

Conversation with:

_____

Aim of the conversation (what needs to be discussed?):

_____

Conversational styles involved:

- Direct
- Indirect
- Both

The impact I hope to have:

_____

_____

Possible meta-message (how will this affect our relationship, or what will this conversation reveal about it?):

_____

_____

Cultural differences to consider:

Motivation for having the conversation (from both sides):

CHAPTER 1 SUMMARY

- In any conversation, there are two key factors to consider: intention and impact. These two don't always align.

  - Intention is the reason for doing something.
  - Impact refers to the outcome based on the actions to fulfill the intention.

- One of the best ways to manage the impact of our intentions is to communicate openly and honestly with those around us.
- Setting intentions upfront is very important, especially for more structured conversations.
- Setting an intention and setting a goal is not the same thing. A conversation should be allowed to flow naturally without a specific goal in mind.

- How we deliver a message could play a role in the impact not matching the intention.
- We can add value to all the conversations we engage in by doing the following:

  ○ Think before we speak.
  ○ Be interested in what the other person is saying.
  ○ Ask questions about the topic.
  ○ Be authentic.
  ○ Keep things specific.
  ○ Build a personal connection by sharing.
  ○ Stay positive.
  ○ Practice active listening.
  ○ Pay attention to our body language as well as theirs.

The next chapter talks about the importance of conversations in creating meaningful relationships, which always occur when the intentions behind each interaction are set right. Read the next chapter to explore how intentions can give meaning to our relationships.

DEVELOPING MEANINGFUL RELATIONSHIPS

If civilization is to survive, we must cultivate the science of human relationships—the ability of all peoples, of all kinds, to live together, in the same world at peace.

— FRANKLIN D. ROOSEVELT

Creating and maintaining relationships can be really hard work, and some people might feel that it's not worth the effort. The more you work on the relationship to create a better bond, the more work you need to put in to maintain it. So why do we do it? Why are relationships so important, and can we live without them?

The short answer to the last question is yes; however, there is a but.

Yes, *but* we will never live a fulfilling and happy life if we are all alone. This doesn't mean that we need a life partner to make the most of it. Friendships and great relationships with family members also count!

Although my older brother and I became the best of friends, it wasn't always like that. In fact, when I was very young, it felt like we were mortal enemies! We were always at each other's necks and competing with each other.

One experience comes to mind that I will never forget. It was a cool, overcast day in the fall. I couldn't have been any older than eight years old. I vividly remember when we were both assigned to do yard work one day, and somehow it became a battle royale! Neither one of us liked yard work. And in our minds, what we were assigned was the worst kind: picking weeds! So, we were already primed for conflict.

One sharp word led to another, and next thing I knew, I was holding a metal rake over my head and threatening my older brother's life! You might be asking yourself, "Why the metal rake?" Was I just psychotic? Wll, that is still up for debate.

All jokes aside, as I said, he was older and bigger than I was. My resourcefulness kicked in, and I was determined to win the battle that day. So, I chose the closest weapon I could find. (Normally, I lost to him at every game we played. So, I was keenly aware of my odds of success.)

What happened after I raised the rake of death?

We'll come back to that later.

The main thing of note is that sometimes because we don't understand or appreciate each other, it can cause conflict. Perhaps there's someone you see or pass by regularly, and you have this feeling there might be a friendship there if only one of you would take the first step. But it never happens. Or you might currently dislike someone, and if you stop and think about it, the reason is very small and insignificant.

Can you think of someone that fits that description?

By learning how to communicate effectively, we can start to overcome differences and build strong and lasting friendships with others. Or it will improve a close relationship you already have with someone.

Another benefit is that we can begin to feel a greater sense of belonging, not only in our own circle, but humanity as a whole (Nash, 2020). With that being said, it takes a lot of hard work to maintain any relationship and still get value from it in the long run.

But how does one go from meeting someone for the first time to developing a meaningful relationship? Not everyone will vibe with you from the get-go, and you both might be missing out on a great friendship simply because the first interaction was not what you anticipated. Or perhaps you desperately want to get to know them better, but they don't seem to feel the same way. What can you do?

COMMUNICATION AND MANIPULATION

First, let's talk about what we *don't* want to do to make friends. One of the biggest mistakes someone can make is using manipulation to get others to like them or return their messages or texts. Contrary to popular belief, we should avoid any form of manipulation when trying to communicate effectively and develop meaningful relationships. And yet, most of the tips and tricks taught online to get others to talk to you involve some form of manipulation.

What does it look like when someone is manipulating someone else, how are we unknowingly manipulating those around us, and how can we avoid it all together? It's difficult to avoid manipulation in a relationship if we don't understand its different forms. Let's take a closer look at some of the aspects related to manipulation.

Manipulation and How It Differs From Communication

Manipulation is a way of tricking someone into doing something we want them to do. In communication, it's tricking them into talking to us either in general or about a specific topic. How? Manipulation focuses on two main aspects: fear and seduction. The one person creates a fear in the other that they might be missing out on something or that they might be holding up a process, when in reality it's not true. The seduction part is someone coercing another into having a conversation or into calling or texting the other person back.

While manipulation is grounded in fear and seduction, true communication focuses on the feelings of the other person, including their worries, the circumstances they find themselves in, and their goals in life.

Take, for example, a scammer who uses the technique of playing on someone's need for consistency. Under normal circumstances, people will try to follow through with what they said, or they will try to appear to be a person of their word. Some scammers will take advantage of this principle of human behavior. Sadly, they have been known to prey on the elderly.

They may say something like,

> Hello, I'm calling from ABC corp. I just wanted to follow up on our conversation from last week (that never happened) and finalize the deal we agreed to. Now I know we wouldn't want to hold up the process because that would be bad for everyone. We're almost finished with the details, but we seem to have missed a digit from your credit card number. It's our mistake. But can you please repeat the card number? That way, we can have everything completed on file.

You might be thinking, *How could anyone fall for this?* Sadly, it happens more than you might think.

I know you, the reader, would never participate in something so vile. But, in principle, we could be doing the same thing, even unknowingly. That's why we want to identify what it can look like, so we avoid it.

It is impossible to build a high value and mutually beneficial relationship using manipulation. Why? Because it involves misusing the trust we've built with someone or taking advantage of their feelings so we can get the result we want. It flows into a short-lived satisfaction and eliminates the possibility of effective collaboration at a later stage.

All of us might consider it at a particular moment and think that it won't do much harm. However, the long-term effects manipulation has on the other person can influence all their future relationships, as well as their self-worth. Not everyone realizes this, which is why it has become one of the "acceptable" ways to get what we want. But is it really acceptable?

Not at all! I think I speak for all of us when I say that we have all been on the wrong side of the stick before. There is also the possibility that we've done it to someone else, again, whether knowingly or unknowingly. It's time we change the norm and start building relationships that last. It is still possible to get a desirable outcome without resorting to manipulation.

What Do Manipulators Do?

There are certain characteristics that most, if not all, manipulators have in common. Below are three specific points that are quite prominent in those who often manipulate others, though there are many other characteristics they might also have.

- **They tend to guilt trip others**: By making others feel guilty about something, even if they haven't done anything wrong, is one of the key skills manipulators possess. It's quite easy to get someone else to do something when they are made to believe they were in the wrong or they owe the manipulator something.
- **They use half-truths**: They tend to choose their words very strategically, relying on half-truths to get them through. Because they are so strategic with what they say, and they choose which side of a story they want to tell, it's often difficult to catch them lying.
- **They have little to no moral boundaries**: There is nothing (or very little) they won't do or say to make sure they get what they want.

Being Unknowingly Manipulative

Whether we mean to be manipulative or not, there are probably a few things that we all currently do or say that can be classified as manipulative. Something as simple as the silent treatment can be considered a type of manipulation.

Manipulation is when we make it hard for the other person to say no, which can easily lead to resentment in a relationship, according to Irina Firstein, a registered therapist (DiValentino, 2017).

Let's look at six habits we tend to develop that could be considered manipulation and how to handle them differently.

The Silent Treatment

Whether we mean to force someone else into apologizing to us by using the silent treatment or not, we love this one. There are two scenarios when this might play out.

The first one is when we don't want to be the first to apologize, so we say nothing and hope that the other person will give in and try to fix the situation first.

The second scenario is out of hurt. When we feel very hurt, we tend to pull away from a relationship to get some distance. Ultimately, this can cause further damage and resentment in the relationship.

What to do:

Respond to these tense situations by taking a short cool-off period and then clear the air. The end goal should always be conflict resolution and the bringing of peace between you and the other person.

Giving Them the Choice but Trying to Influence Their Decision

What does this sound like? We may say something to the effect of: "I trust your judgment, but this car is more fuel efficient and drives faster, and the color is just amazing. But it's your choice."

I know I have been guilty of this one. By positioning something in this manner, we push the other person into a certain direction while trying to make it seem like they have the choice. Whenever we present someone with a choice and then try to convince them that one is better than the other and finish it off by saying it's still up to them, this is a way of manipulating them into choosing what we think is best.

What to do:

It's better to be straightforward and tell them what we would choose and then ask their opinion. Something like, "I really like this car, and I'm definitely leaning more toward it because it appears to be more fuel efficient. What do you think?"

Notice the contrast from the earlier statement. Using phrases like "it seems" or "it appears to be" is not dogmatic. Using absolutes like "it is" in some cases can be manipulative because we're trying to impress upon the other person's mind of a "fact." If we really want the other person to choose, we give them the same info we have and help them make an informed decision.

Having a Pity Party

Having a tantrum when someone hasn't gotten around to doing something that we've asked them to might feel good, as if we have made a point, but it's never the right solution to the problem.

It normally sounds something like: "It's fine. I'll do it myself."

It sounds like an innocent and appropriate response, but it makes the other person feel extremely guilty for not getting around to it yet. Why? Because they might have a valid excuse for not doing it, and by responding this way, we're basically letting them know that the reason they haven't gotten to it yet is irrelevant.

What to do:

First consider whether the task was reasonable and if the other person has had enough time (and the resources) to handle it. When we feel like it was reasonable, we should approach the other person and be direct about what we need from them in a mild and respectable way.

Making Suggestions About Someone Else's Feelings

This might be one of the most common ones and something most of us do on a daily basis.

It could sound something like: "Don't you want to have a drink? Let me get you one."

Instead of asking whether they want one, we are suggesting that they do and covertly making them have one because we want one. Why is this manipulative? Because it essentially makes it seem like having a drink was their idea.

What to do:

In this scenario, simply admit that a drink would be nice and then ask whether they would also like one. This can be applied to anything else, like heading to the gym or going out for dinner.

The Promises We Can't Keep

Overpromising might seem like a good idea when you can benefit from trying to convince someone of something. But isn't that exactly what manipulation is? We might think that it's nothing big. After all, we don't really have control over what does and does not happen. But at the end of the day, if we overpromise and don't deliver on that promise, the other person feels disappointed, and it might hurt the relationship even more.

I've seen this so many times, and I've actually experienced it firsthand. When there is no sign of the promise being fulfilled and the opposite happens, the disappointment is hard to overcome and rectify.

This often happens in love relationships when one person feels like the other person is not carrying their weight, and when confronted, they start making promises just to keep their partner around. Promises like, "I will cook every night and clean the house all by myself." These promises seem very enticing when we are in the moment, and it might convince them to stay. However, when it's time to deliver on the promises and nothing happens, more damage is done to the relationship.

This does not only apply to love relationships. There could also be an incident where we want our partner or a friend to go to a party with us and we overpromise on how epic the party is going to be. (How can we make a promise on something we have no real control over?)

What to do:

Be direct and honest with the person. Have an open conversation with them and give them the facts. If they don't want to do something, we can ask them why and try to understand their hesitance instead of trying to coerce them into doing something they might regret.

Constantly Forgetting to Do Things

It's really late, you might be feeling quite tired from a long day of work, and you don't feel like doing the dishes. You know it's your turn, but you can't get yourself to do them. We've all been there, some of us more often than others. And that's okay.

What's not okay is when it happens consistently and everyone else needs to pick up the slack, whether it's chores at home or work projects and assignments. When it becomes a habit, it places everyone else under more pressure, who might also need to take care of their own responsibilities.

What to do:

Again, be completely honest about it and have a sit-down conversation with those who are most affected by our lack of contribution or effort. Why? Because just talking about it and being forthright is much better received than making repeated excuses.

MEANINGFUL RELATIONSHIPS

What can we do to create and maintain meaningful relationships?

The simple truth is that relationships take hard work. Creating meaningful ones can be quite a challenge, but it's completely worth it. How so? Because in a meaningful relationship, we have the opportunity to build on such qualities as mutual interest, trust, respect, and value between us and someone else. These relationships are so important for overall wellness and living a fulfilling life. Although our smaller differences and unique perspectives keep things interesting, the more we have in common with someone when it comes to our *core values*, the higher the possibility of developing a meaningful relationship.

The problem I think most of us experience is finding the time to maintain these relationships. They're like flowers: You need to tend to them with lots of love and care, and make sure they get a sufficient amount of water and sunlight. Without these efforts, the flower won't survive. The more love and care it receives, the more it will grow and blossom.

So how can we nourish our current relationships?

Qualities of Meaningful Relationships

I recently started an exercise routine at home. At the time of writing this book, I now work out, on average, every other day. I've exercised before and stopped after some time. And then it dawned on me one day that there's no real merit in exercising one or two days and then stopping. This led me to the conclusion that one of the greatest "muscles" to exercise is **consistency**. With that being said, let's go over some vital qualities for developing meaningful relationships. And that, if done repeatedly, adds lasting value to it.

Communication

We use communication to share ideas and connect with each other. None of the characteristics below will be possible without open communication, making it a cornerstone to any relationship. When a relationship starts to deteriorate, communication is most often the first thing that's affected.

Communication can be verbal and nonverbal, and both of these are important in relationships.

What to do:

Always be honest and clear about our thoughts, feelings, and intentions, and give the other person room to do the same.

Dependability

To be dependable means that when you say you will do something, no one has to wonder whether you will. You always keep your word. It's very closely linked to honesty, which we discuss further down. By being dependable, we're sending the message that we'll always be there and support the other person in the relationship.

What to do:

Make sure that when we say we're going to do something, we get it done, regardless of the obstacles we might face. (Of course, what we say we are going to do must be reasonable in the first place.)

Empathy

A whole chapter in my book, *Help Me, I'm Stuck*, is dedicated to applying empathy. With good reason. Why? Because empathy does not come naturally to everyone, and some of us might need to put in a bit more work to come across as empathetic than others.

While sympathy is feeling sorry for the other person, empathy is the ability "to walk a mile in another man's moccasins," as a native American proverb says. It shows great support to the other person and makes them feel valued and understood.

What to do:

When someone expresses their thoughts or feelings, listen to them and acknowledge their experience. Once we understand where they're coming from, we will also know whether they wanted us to respond or if they just needed to talk to someone.

Honesty

If I had to ask you to name one of the most important aspects of a relationship, would you agree that trust is somewhere at the top? Without honesty, a relationship will have a serious lack of trust. Without trust, there won't be much of a relationship, which is why it is so important. Our words and actions should always align with each other.

What to do:

Speak honestly with others even when it's difficult to do. (This should also be balanced with discretion.)

Interdependence

To be interdependent means that we are not approaching life like a lone wolf. We realize that while we're always putting our best foot forward, there are times that we will need help from others.

What to do:

Accept help from others.

Purpose

There's always a purpose for any given relationship. There is a reason you started talking to each other and sharing ideas. By having a purpose, it's clear for both parties what is expected of them in the relationship and what is seen as appropriate behavior. Without purpose, there is no value.

Purpose is the age-old "What is this?" discussion that should be had (unless it's obvious, such as a work relationship).

What to do:

It would be wise to define the purpose of a relationship in the beginning stages. Why? So both parties will be clear about the nature of a relationship so that expectations are met and boundaries are respected. If the dynamic is changing between two parties, the purpose of the relation-ship should be re-evaluated when circumstances change.

Respect

Respect is to regard someone else's being, ideas, thoughts, and feelings positively and in high esteem. It doesn't mean agreeing all the time with others but allowing them to keep their dignity, even if they're wrong. It's pivotal to any rela-tionship as it goes hand-in-hand with interdependence and honesty.

Showing respect is something that most of us have been taught since a very young age, although we might not have linked the act to respect. Has anyone ever told you to treat others the way you want to be treated? That's respect. (This saying also points to the need to respect ourselves. We can more easily respect ourselves if we practice the qualities above.)

What to do:

Pretend that showing respect is like a game. The rules are simple. Whoever displays it first is the winner!

The Importance of Meaningful Connections

When we manage to develop meaningful connections with others, it helps us to thrive in all areas of our lives. How? Well, there are quite a few benefits of developing these connections, such as improved self-worth and confidence, better resilience, and better mental health, to name a few.

According to Louis Cozolino, who is a psychology professor at Pepperdine University, meaningful relationships have the biggest impact on the brain and longevity, promoting healthy brain function and a sense of purpose in life (The Importance of Meaningful Relationships, 2020). Developing meaningful relationships can reduce the rate in which our brains age.

The more social we are and the more we relate to others, the higher our chances will be of living longer and having a more fulfilling life. It's amazing how our bodies work. When we have a strong connection with someone or a few people, it decreases the chances of serious medical conditions, such as heart attacks and mental disorders. This is because the people around us, and our relationship with them, influences our physical and psychological health more than we may realize.

Barriers to Meaningful Connections

It's worth mentioning that there are a few barriers that we should look out for and manage when developing these meaningful relationships.

Some of these barriers we create ourselves, while others are a result of life happening. It's how we deal with the barriers we encounter that will determine whether the connection will survive or not. What should we do?

Being Vulnerable Is Tough

Vulnerability is an important aspect of forming meaningful relationships. That being said, it's an absolutely terrifying thought to be completely vulnerable with someone, especially when that same vulnerability has hurt you in the past.

Something very special happens when we feel comfortable enough to share some of our deepest fears, goals, and dreams with another person. When someone else can see that we are being completely real and vulnerable, they automatically feel connected to us.

What to do:

Allow yourself to voluntarily be seen as weak. This will actually draw people to you.

Just Not Caring

It shouldn't happen too often, but sometimes it's really difficult to get ourselves to care enough to pursue a connection with someone else. It's the "If it happens, it happens. If it doesn't, oh well," kind of attitude that we seem to adopt if things haven't quite gone our way recently.

It's a dangerous place to be, and we should address and fix it as soon as we become aware of it. How can we fix it?

What to do:

Take a day off, de-stress, or play with kittens (or watch them on YouTube, which always makes me feel better). There are very few emotional problems that kittens can't solve. Slim to none.

Our Busy Schedules

It's no secret that we've become busier over the years. Most of us have a full-time job, as well as one or a few side hustles just to make a living. Our schedules can make it quite difficult to connect with others because, honestly, after a long day at work and taking care of all my other responsibilities, the last thing I want to do is entertain someone. I want to relax on the sofa, get lost in a book, and just forget about the busy day.

The problem is that this affects our relationships in such a negative way that it could be hard to recover from that. Although we are all busy after a long day, chasing these connections and making sure that the other person feels valued and understood is so important.

This also goes for relationships where we might only see the person once a week or once a month. Maybe there's a standing arrangement for breakfast every Saturday morning but getting out of bed is a struggle after a long week at work.

If the other person can make an effort, then so can we! And I'm definitely talking to myself here too. I have been guilty of canceling plans at the last minute because I was just too tired to go. The problem with this is that once you've done it the first time, it's easy to do it again.

What to do:

Show up. That's all the other person expects of us. Be dependable and be there for them when you reasonably can.

Our Filtering Process

Our filtering process is quite important to avoid information overload, but it can be a huge barrier when forming connections.

In short, our filtering process is where we filter the information we receive and decide what is important to remember and what should be ignored or discarded. Something as small as the other person's favorite color might not make the cut in terms of important information, but when it comes to building meaningful relationships, these small details make all the difference.

What to do:

Remember small details about the other person. Why? They will be reassured that we care about them and value what they say.

Technology

Technology can either improve our connections or ultimately sever them. It really depends on how we use it.

For those struggling to connect with others, technology gives us the opportunity to get to know other people without the social pressures we may feel in a room full of people. When physical meetings are impossible, technology helps us get in touch with those who are most important to us virtually to ensure the relationship doesn't suffer due to life happening. If you think back to when COVID-19 just started and the whole world went into lockdown, our friendships and mental health would not have survived if we didn't have technology.

My grandparents, who are both approaching 90 years old, are amazing examples of making an effort. During the pandemic, in an effort to stay connected with my family all over the states, a group of 10 or so arranged to meet on Zoom every week. Although technology was challenging for them, my grandparents were taught by my sister and brother-in-law how to work an iPad and use Zoom. They consistently met every week for over a year! Words cannot express how special it was to see them, especially knowing the effort it took for them to get on the call.

On the flip side, a lot of people use technology as an escape mechanism from the real world. They get so engrossed in another world that they completely disregard and neglect the people around them. They forget to nurture and grow the relationships they already have. Technology can be such a big distraction for us, and we need to make sure that we're using it for the right reasons while still paying attention to those who we can physically connect with.

What to do:

Set aside time to contact those who you would like to keep in touch with. Choose a day and an hour that works for you both and follow through.

LET'S BE HONEST...

Now to return to the deadly rake story at the beginning of the chapter!

I'm very glad to say that right before I swiped at my brother, my mother got involved and broke us up. And boy, were we in trouble! We both got the spanking of a lifetime, and I really think that was a turning point for us.

As the years went by, I learned that he really cared for me. And, as expected from a younger brother, I admired him in many ways and wanted to be just like him. More than that, we developed mutual respect for each other. And this relationship grew stronger and stronger every year. We relied on and trusted each other very much. It is a uniquely satisfying and fulfilling experience.

The truth is, you might have a potential friend right in front of you! And the more we take the time to see the other person for who they are, we come to appreciate there's something special and unique about them. I truly believe each human being on this planet is superior to me in one way or another and that I would, in some way, learn from them if the opportunity presents itself. Not only that, but they're not so different from us. They might even make a good friend. Or, like what my older brother became to me, a *best* friend.

And now that we've covered the basics on communication and meaningful relationships, below I have listed a few questions for you. The point is to be completely honest with yourself. No one is going to check your answers and rate them. This is for your eyes only.

To get the best out of this exercise, write down your answers and then revisit the questions once you have completed this book. You might be surprised how much you've grown through the chapters!

1. Do you find it easy to talk to new people and make friends?

2. Do you know how to make friends?

3. Do you know what to talk about when you first meet someone?

4. Are you able to keep a conversation going?

5. If something goes wrong between you and someone else, is it easy for you to pinpoint what it is and what caused it?

6. Do you know how to fix things when it starts going wrong? Or how to bring up an issue to talk about it?

7. If you're in a conversation with someone new and you feel unsafe, what would you do?

8. Is there someone in your life that you can talk to about anything?

CHAPTER 2 SUMMARY

- Developing meaningful relationships with those around us cultivates a sense of belonging and purpose.
- One of the main factors that prevent us from developing these meaningful relationships is manipulation.
- Most of us can fall into the manipulation trap from a giving and receiving perspective. It's important that we pay attention to how we communicate with others and how they communicate with us.
- High-quality relationships include open communication, dependability, empathy, honesty, interdependence, purpose, and respect.
- We should aim to always add value and pursue these meaningful connections.

The next chapter talks about the skills of listening and the importance thereof in communication.

LISTENING IS ABOUT MORE THAN JUST SOUNDS

Remember when we were young and our parents or another adult used to read to us? Whether it was a once-in-a-while occurrence or every day, these experiences were likely some of our fondest memories.

Did you know there are many benefits of reading to young children? You probably can think of a few. Not only do they help with bonding and developing a relationship, but it also helps children develop their listening skills. Children learn to listen intently to what is being said and create an image in their minds based on the words they are hearing. It helps to let their imagination run wild and allow them the space to develop their own thoughts and ideas.

That is, if they are *actually* listening.

One day when I was in elementary school, my class went on a field trip. There were clear blue skies, and the sun was shining very brightly. For our classroom, it was one of the best kinds of field trips: a nature exploration! On our way there, the bus was filled with excitement. What would we see? When we arrived, we were led to a small room with many pictures of animals and plants. A nature guide was chosen to guide and teach us. She read from a book that explained the fascinating lives of...

The fascinating lives of...

Oh, that's right. I wasn't listening. I was distracted by my classmates who had checked out and became unapologetically disruptive. I'll never forget what happened next because it was massively embarrassing.

We'll come back to that story later.

Listening is a skill we can foster from a very young age, and we should never neglect it when trying to improve ourselves. Why? Because no matter how interesting something is that someone else is telling us, there is always the temptation to give into distraction.

Can you remember a situation where you were talking to someone, and it was clear that they were distracted? Although they were making eye contact and nodding at everything you said, you could clearly see that they were not listening. They asked questions you had already answered and interrupted you while you were speaking, thinking they knew how your sentence was ending. It's a horrible feeling.

Now think about a time when someone paid attention to what you were saying and took in every word. You could see them making mental notes about some things, and although they also nodded and kept eye contact like the other person, you could tell they were genuinely interested in the conversation.

Which one of the two would you rather speak to again?

THE IMPORTANCE OF LISTENING

"Are you even listening?"

Does that sound familiar? I hope not. But in today's day and age, we are so consumed with everything going on around us and with technology pulling us in different directions, we have forgotten what it means to really listen to someone.

A key component to developing meaningful relationships and effectively communicating with others is to be able to listen with the intent to understand, not necessarily respond.

Listening does not come naturally to all, but there are a few things we can do to practice and develop this skill. These are mainly habits we can integrate into our daily lives; we will explore this later in the chapter. Let's first cover some of the basics when it comes to listening.

Hearing vs Listening

There's a big difference between hearing and listening. Maybe your parents pointed this out to you at one time or another when you forgot to wash the dishes (like my parents did). Anyone can hear something, but it takes additional effort to actually listen. If I know I'm about to talk to someone, I have a secret weapon that primes my mindset to be a better listener. What is it? I pretend that whoever is speaking to me is, one, the most important person in the world, and two, that whatever they are talking about is a matter of life and death. Does that sound extreme? It all depends on how good of a listener you want to be!

When we listen, we apply our minds and ensure that we are hearing the information, digesting it and processing it, in an attempt to understand what is being said. The experience of talking to someone who hears what we say versus talking to someone who actually listens are worlds apart.

Here are some of the biggest differences between hearing and listening:

Hearing	Listening
Done automatically and happens within the moment.	A skill that is learned and mastered through practice over time.
We don't need to focus to be able to hear something. In fact, sometimes we might even hear things we weren't supposed to.	You can't listen to someone accidently. It takes effort and concentration to actually listen to what someone else is saying.
An involuntary action with no effort required.	So voluntary. So, so voluntary. Without the intention to do so, listening does not happen at all.

Benefits of Listening

Practicing active listening has a myriad of benefits, including:

- The ability to better sympathize and empathize with those around us.
- Improving the ability to understand certain concepts in a personal and professional capacity.
- The ability to make others feel listened to and valued, which also results in better relationship bonds.

Can you imagine how much better life would be if you improved each of these abilities?

Listening Styles

Did you know there are different styles of listening? People listen in different ways, and it's important to understand which style you have and how you can adapt, depending on who you're listening to. Why is this important to understand? Because when we are the speaker, knowing our style will prevent any type of misunderstandings. For example, some listeners need the speaker to repeat certain things to aid their understanding and help them to remember, but for others, it may seem rude.

The following are the three main styles of listening.

Content

Listeners who fall within this category are very focused on the content of the message. They want to know and understand the details, make sense of it, and make sure that it's accurate. They want all the information, and no detail is too small. They like receiving new information and learning from others.

People

These listeners are often seen as very empathetic as they are very interested in the other person, including their thoughts and feelings surrounding what they are sharing.

As an example, someone with this listening style who is watching an interview of a famous artist will be more interested to learn about the artist's background and childhood than their actual art. Although they might appreciate the art, their focus is more on the person and not what the person brings to the table.

These kinds of listeners run the risk of missing the message because they are too focused on the person. They might be thinking of questions they could ask the artist to get to know them rather than listening to what the person is saying.

Time

These listeners have no time for beating around the bush. They want the other person to make their point as soon as possible without long-winded explanations and stories. They easily become impatient when someone explains something in a roundabout way. It's easy to spot their impatience by looking at their body language as they will start fiddling, looking around, shifting in their seat, etc.

Which style do you identify with?

The Process of Listening

Many studies have been done to understand what goes into the process of listening. The following are the five steps of listening. It seems like a long-winded approach that could take a few hours or days to complete, but it happens within seconds.

Receiving

This is the most fundamental step to listening. Getting it wrong at this step will impact the rest of the process.

Receiving involves taking in the information provided by the other person. Verbal and nonverbal information can be given, and as the listeners, we should be receptive to all information provided. Having complete focus and avoiding distractions are key to this step. Although one should never interrupt the other person while they are sharing information, it is especially important during this first step.

Understanding

In this step, we now need to understand the information that was provided so that we can come up with an appropriate response. The actual response only happens later, but we need to make sure that we have enough information and that we understand it in order to formulate a response.

Remembering

Although this might seem similar to the previous two steps, it's actually different. Here, the aim is to capture and understand the information in our minds. It might be impossible to capture this word for word, so the best approach is to store keywords from the conversation that highlight the important bits.

Just remembering it for a short period of time is not the goal here. When listening, we need to ensure that we are storing the information away in long-term memory so that it's easily accessible when we need it again in the future.

Because many people today have an untrained memory, it's best we don't rely solely on our ability to bring up details in our mind. Using a calendar or notepad immediately after receiving certain kinds of information is invaluable to becoming a better listener.

Evaluating

Evaluating the information before responding is very important. During this stage, we decide what an appropriate response will be and whether a response is even required. We should ask ourselves questions like:

- What was the person's intention for sharing this with me?
- Are they looking for a solution, or are they just looking for someone to listen?
- Have we had a similar conversation before, and what was the outcome?

Responding

Once all of these are in place, responding to the other person should be relatively easy. We should be careful not to disregard anything the person is saying and acknowledge their thoughts and feelings, even if we disagree with them.

If all of this seems easy, that's because it is. Actually, listening is not that difficult. The difficult part is putting in the effort to do it.

The Barriers to Listening

There can be quite a few reasons why we don't listen sometimes. This includes simple things like distractions in the environment and our short attention span.

Other things may also play a role, like thinking we know what the other person will say before they say it, so we start thinking about a response instead of listening to them. All of us have been guilty of this at one point or another.

Let's discuss two barriers in more detail.

Distractions

It's always important that we eliminate all distractions when having an important conversation so that we're able to focus on the discussion. This includes physical distractions in the environment, as well as our own distractions in our minds. For example, avoiding the temptation to check our phones while someone is speaking. If a person is being vulnerable with us and pouring their heart out, we shouldn't be wondering what we're going to make for dinner tonight or thinking about a conversation with someone else earlier that day.

Being completely present in the moment and giving them our full attention is a great way to let them know that they are important to us, that we care about them, and that we'll be there for them when they might need us most.

Attention Span

This ties back to distraction as well. Sometimes, we can be our worst enemies. It's easy to stop listening if something doesn't particularly interest us. The problem is that the other person will pick up on it as soon as we lose interest in the conversation and make a note to never share that part of their lives with us again.

Something that works for me is trying to relate it back to something I like or find interesting. Or just observing how happy it makes them to talk about their interests. I always find new motivation to listen when I see how passionate they are about what they're talking about.

How to Improve Your Listening Skills

There are always ways to improve our listening skills. Let's look at a few. Later in this chapter, we will also focus on what active listening is and how to improve it.

Fact or Opinion

We should spot the difference between fact and opinion. We tend to form our own beliefs about certain things, which create our biases. When someone decides to engage in a conversation with us about these, we might focus on our own opinions instead of the facts related to the topic.

What to do:

Always look at the facts when listening to others and not base our response, or our listening efforts, on any opinions we may have on the matter. Why? This will help us to stay objective and we can add the most value to the conversation.

Get Rid of Assumptions

We need to always try to push our own assumptions aside. These could be detrimental to listening and being on the sharing side of the conversation.

One of the best pieces of advice I've received regarding this point is to get out of my own mind. My anxiety would tell me that when I ask someone too many questions, they might think I'm nosy. That's an assumption I make up all by myself without any facts to back it up.

How about from the other side?

Can you tell the difference between when someone is just asking questions to fill the time and when they are genuinely interested in what you're saying?

If we keep allowing our fear of how someone will react to prevent us from having meaningful conversations, we'll never be able to create those amazing interactions with others.

What to do:

Don't be afraid to ask more questions to learn about what someone is telling you, and have the intention to understand what they are saying. Exercise discernment with your questions and make adjustments based on how close you are to the other person. But generally, if you are coming from a sincere place, people will see that you are just trying to take a personal interest in them.

Take Notes

If we are having an important conversation with someone, especially when it's professional, it's okay to take notes. This helps us to remember what was said and reflect on the points raised. There is no need to take down everything they say but noting down key points and next steps are important to ensure expectations are met.

What to do:

Use your phone, notepad, and/or calendar to jot down important points from a conversation during or after you both have finished talking.

ACTIVE LISTENING

Most of us are not active listeners by default. This is something we need to focus on and improve if we want to get the best out of our conversations. We should be fully present, take in everything they say, and then process that information to understand what the other person is trying to tell us and their intention behind sharing this information (instead of just hearing the general message they are conveying).

How to Improve Active Listening

Using the above points and some additional tips, let's explore what they mean and how we can improve our active listening.

Nonverbal Cues

Most of our communication is in the form of nonverbal cues, and when we don't pay attention to these, we might miss more than half of what the other person is trying to say. It's important to pay attention to any nonverbal cues as these could tell us a lot about what the person is going through. They might come across as cool, calm, and collected, but they speak really fast or avoid eye contact. This could mean that they're feeling really anxious, but they're trying not to make it too obvious.

Nonverbal body language is important from a listener's side as well. When we are the listener, we should ensure that our body language is open and nonthreatening. The person should know that we're not there to judge them and that we're listening to what they're saying.

What to do:

Smile while the other person is speaking (if the message allows) and nod every now and then. Using hand gestures, especially where the palms can be seen, portrays trustworthiness to the listener. These are great ways to put others at ease and keep a conversation going.

Avoid Judgment

The last thing the other person needs is for us to judge them, especially when it's a difficult and sensitive topic.

What to do:

Remain neutral in your responses to keep the other person from shutting down. This will encourage them to share more.

Use Patience

This can be really difficult, but it involves listening to understand their intent and the information instead of just listening to respond. We should never interrupt someone while they're speaking. Even if there are some silences, we shouldn't attempt to respond to anything that has been said until the other person has shared everything they wanted.

What to do:

During the brief silences, give a word of encouragement or ask an open-ended question. This can be used to get the conversation going again.

Be Present

Just sitting in front of someone and nodding every now and then does not mean that we are fully present in the moment. Being fully present means that the other person has our undivided attention and that we are using all of our senses to listen to and understand what they're trying to say.

What to do:

Stop worrying about what happened earlier in the day. Do not think about the problems you're currently facing. Avoid trying to finish their sentences for them and don't start to formulate a response before they've had a chance to properly express themselves.

Reflect and Paraphrase

This is an important part of a conversation where we should be paraphrasing what we heard to ensure we understand what they said. This helps to avoid any possible miscommunication as they can immediately point out anything that we may have missed.

What to do:

Starting a response with, "So, it seems like what you're saying is..." or "It sounds like you think that..." are great ways to paraphrase information back. Asking, "Did I get that right?" is an excellent way to get confirmation that you're both on the same page.

Eye Contact

This is a sign that we're listening to everything the other person is saying without caring about any possible distractions (which is not always true, as I will illustrate in the second half of my story at the end of this chapter). By maintaining genuine eye contact, we immediately make the person feel like we're really there to listen to what they have to say.

With that being said, eye contact can be a little weird if it's too intense.

What to do:

A great rule of thumb is to maintain eye contact for around four to five seconds at a time and then look away for a few seconds before making eye contact again.

Open-Ended Questions

Open-ended questions are when the other person needs to respond with more than just a "yes" or "no." By using these questions in a conversation, we allow the interaction to flow. The other person can then choose how much information they would like to share based on the question.

What to do:

Ask open-ended questions. This shows that we are interested in what the other person is saying, and we would like to know more about it. Here are some example questions you can try:

- What outcome are you hoping to achieve?
- What are your thoughts on this?
- How can I support you during this journey?
- Can you elaborate on this a little more?

Practice Makes Perfect

As mentioned before, active listening is a skill. The only way to get better at something and improve our skills is to practice. We should practice our active listening every chance we get. Soon it will become second nature.

What to do:

Don't give up! If you feel that, after practicing these suggestions, you're not doing a good job, it's because it's probably true. And that's ok. Before you are great, you have to be good. And before you're good, sometimes you have to be terrible at a new thing you're doing. Just keep trying. Consistent effort is key!

Talk About Something Interesting

There is nothing worse than trying to make conversation with someone who wants to talk about something we are not interested in. Finding common interests will help get both parties excited about the conversation and really lean in.

What to do:

My highest suggestion in this regard is to be well read. Read books about topics you are interested in. Learn more about something you're curious about. Try out a new novel. Sharing these topics with someone else is truly an amazing feeling!

Rounding Things Off

Now to finish the story from earlier in this chapter. Sadly, the guide had totally lost the attention of the rest of the class. In a strong effort to be polite, I kept my gaze fixed on the speaker but to no avail. Why? Although my eyes were on the guide as she tried to read from the book she had chosen, I understood nothing from the words coming out of her mouth. I allowed the distraction from the rest of the children to consume my attention.

Here's the embarrassing part: She asked me to repeat back what she said. As you might expect, I had nothing to say. I just smiled and shamefully shook my head.

Of course, I was young and hadn't trained my listening skills at the time. If you feel yourself getting the urge to let your thoughts wander while someone is talking or get distracted by something else, remember the points above and practice them regularly. It's also okay to let the person speaking know that right now might not be the best time because you have so much on your mind. In this case, we could always request to speak about it at a different time when you can give them 100% of your attention, as was mentioned above. This shows a great deal of respect for the speaker.

CHAPTER 3 SUMMARY

- There is a big difference between hearing something someone is saying and actively listening to someone.
- By practicing active listening, we can make someone else feel valued and heard.
- Just like everything else in life, there is a process to listening. This process happens within seconds and consists of receiving, understanding, remembering, evaluating, and responding.
- We might have difficulty listening to someone if we experience any barriers in communication. These barriers can be internal and external.
- Active listening involves listening to the other person with intention and purpose: To understand their point of view and respond in a way that adds value to the exchange.
- We can improve our active listening skills with practice.

The next chapter talks about the barriers to effective communication.

THE ROADBLOCKS IN COMMUNICATION

Have you ever been so caught up with your own thoughts and feelings, reflecting on the day and making plans for tomorrow, that you found it nearly impossible to engage in a conversation with a friend or significant other? Perhaps you were there in the beginning, but the longer the conversation went on, the less you actually listened.

It's happened more times to me than I would like to admit. The important thing is to admit that it is a problem and then work to fix it.

One of my friends confided in me about this exact issue before. He got home after a long day at work where everything seemed to go wrong. He was frustrated and tired and just wanted to put his feet up and relax. Out of habit, he asked his wife how her day was. Unfortunately, the day's events and what awaited him at work the next day were playing on his mind so much that he didn't listen to what she was telling him. He encountered a communication roadblock.

Did this backfire on him at all? We'll save the ending for later.

For now, we can focus on this point: Encountering road-blocks is a part of life. It helps us to grow and improve and become a better version of ourselves than we were yesterday. Without roadblocks, we may not feel the need to improve ourselves.

In this chapter, we will look at some of the roadblocks we may encounter when it comes to effective communication and how to overcome them to allow conversations to flow easily.

BARRIERS TO EFFECTIVE COMMUNICATION

Barriers in communication can cause miscommunication and lead to conflict in relationships. There are a number of barriers that exist, and some are more common than others.

Communication barriers can be classified as anything that prevents the receiver from receiving and understanding the message the way it was intended. These barriers can exist during various stages of communication: from the sender, from the interpretation of the message, from the receiver, or from the feedback.

Cultural Barriers

Certain cultures have set rules for interacting and communicating with others. For example, in some cultures it may be frowned upon for a man and a woman who are not married to hug. In other cultures, this is completely normal.

These cultural differences may cause barriers in conversation if they are not known and properly understood.

Emotional Barriers

Depending on how close we are to someone, speaking about something really emotional and being vulnerable is very difficult. Some people also have a harder time talking about their feelings and expressing their opinion on something, which could cause animosity if the one person shares more than the other.

Most of us also have topics that we prefer to avoid, and when the other person brings it up, this could also create barriers in the conversation.

Linguistic Barriers

Linguistic barriers include not only language but different dialects as well. Even if someone speaks the same language as us, it's easy to misunderstand what they said if they have a different dialect or accent than ours.

Perception Barriers

We all have our own perception of specific things in life. These perceptions have been formed based on our experiences, culture, upbringing, morals and values, and other environmental factors. When these perceptions differ from the people we have conversations with, this could create a barrier that is hard to overcome.

Attitude barriers also fall within this category, as it deals with our perceptions about a situation.

Physical Communication Barriers

This involves communication over text or the phone, where we can't physically see the other person. Nonverbal communication plays an important role in effective communication, and this is impossible to read through text.

Physiological Barriers

There are some physical disabilities that could create barriers in conversation, such as partial or complete hearing loss or even speech disabilities.

Prejudice Barriers

Preconceived ideas and notions are common. We often use the stereotypes and assumptions we've made over the years to filter out what information we are willing to receive and what information to block out completely. By blocking out some information, we might miss the bigger picture.

Psychological Barriers

Our mental state at the time we received the message can make a difference in how we perceive it. If we are stressed out or feeling down, we will comprehend the message in a different manner than when we are having a good day.

Those with mental disorders, such as anxiety and depression, can also experience a message very differently to those who are just having a bad day.

OVERCOMING BARRIERS

Let's take a look at some of the ways we can effectively overcome these barriers.

Clear Ideas

We need to organize and make sense of the ideas we want to communicate before sharing them with other people. This involves going over the ideas in your mind and making sure that you completely understand what you need to say.

What I like to do is preempt some of the questions that the other person might ask during the conversation, and then I make sure that I have a ready answer for it. By asking these questions to myself, it helps to crystalize the idea even more.

Content, Language, Tone

These should all be aligned to the actual message and presented and customized in relation to who will receive it.

It may be difficult to keep a neutral tone when delivering bad news or reprimanding someone for something, but using a tone that might hurt the other person may lead to them shutting down and creating a barrier in the conversation. Content and language should also be fit for purpose.

Feedback

While communicating, we should pay attention to the feedback we receive to determine whether the person who got the message understood what we said. We could ask them to repeat what they understand or pick up on nonverbal cues during the conversation.

Follow Up

If it was an important conversation where an action needed to be taken, we should follow up with the receiver to ensure they are still on track and understand what is expected. We all forget sometimes and need a reminder to push us in the right direction.

Keeping the Receiver's Needs in Mind

We're not all on the same level and can't communicate with each other the same. For example, the way you speak to an adult and the words you use during a conversation are worlds apart from when you speak to a five-year-old child.

Creating a message specific to the audience and their needs will prevent anything going over their heads or bringing them any unnecessary or elementary information.

Make Sure It's Helpful

By including interesting and helpful information that draws the other person in, we can keep them engaged in the conversation for a longer period of time. People invest time into something when they are interested in it or know that they will benefit from it.

Practice Active Listening

Refer back to the previous chapter to read more on active listening, why it's important, and how to be an active listener.

Use a Sounding Board

In situations where we're not sure whether the message is fit for purpose or whether we're explaining it correctly, using someone else as a sounding board can be very helpful. This should be someone we trust and who will be completely honest about the delivery of the message.

LEARN FROM HIS MISTAKE

So, how did things end with my friend? His wife told him that she got a promotion at work, but he missed that piece of information while he was lost in his own thoughts. When she told her parents over the phone later that same evening, he was upset that she didn't tell him first. Of course, she did, but because he allowed his own thoughts to block out their conversation, he had no recollection of her telling him.

Of course, you and I want to avoid having that outcome as much as possible. It's understanding to make a mistake, but even better to be aware and try to avoid them. Above, you've learned how to avoid making the same errors in your personal life. What else can help?

Use the worksheet on the following page to identify barriers that you can work on in your relationships.

WORKING ON MYSELF WORKSHEET

Reflect on the barriers discussed earlier in the chapter and identify how these may play a role in your current relationships. At the end of the worksheet, write down some of the ways you are trying to overcome these barriers or measures you are planning to put in place for the future.

Cultural Barriers	Emotional Barriers	Linguistic Barriers	Perception Barriers

Physical Barriers	Physiological Barriers	Prejudice Barriers	Psychological Barriers

Measures already in place to manage these:

_____

_____

_____

_____

_____

What I plan on putting in place in the near future:

_____

_____

_____

_____

_____

Before we continue, I would like you to stop reading this book for a few minutes to help someone else overcome these barriers.

Someone who also struggles with effective communication, just like you, and who has tried everything to get better but with little to no success. You've probably never met this person before, but right now they need this book as much as you do, if not even more. Taking just a few minutes to write a quick review will help them find my book, just like you did.

Here's how you do it: If you are listening to this book on Audible, tap the three dots in the top right of your device, click "rate and review," and write a few sentences about my book. And don't forget to rate it: From one to five, you can choose how many stars you feel my book deserves.

If you are reading on Kindle or another e-reader, just scroll to the bottom of the book, swipe up, and you will be prompted to leave a review.

If any features have changed on your reading app, please use your receipt to find the link to my book on Amazon, and simply leave a review right there.

Thank you so much for your help—and for paying it forward by doing something good for someone else without expecting anything in return. As soon as you've written your review, be sure to come right back so you can start with the next chapter.

CHAPTER 4 SUMMARY

- We can experience various barriers in communication—some formed by our own experiences and biases, and some formed through the environment and cultural differences.
- To ensure that we communicate effectively with those around us, it's important to identify and have a plan to overcome any barriers that may come up.

The next chapter talks about the basic elements of conversation.

BASICS OF CONVERSATION

Imagine having a conversation with someone who makes you feel like they really care and value what you're saying. They don't try to interrupt you, force their opinions or biases on you, or judge you in any way. Whenever you share something important with them, they take it to heart and try to help in any way they can. They also tend to remember important things, such as your nephew's soccer game that was coming up, and they ask you about it later on.

They're charismatic and fun, and every time they make time to talk to you, it instantly makes your day better. This person is someone that everyone yearns to talk to, yet they choose you. Every time you two have a conversation, you meditate and reflect on it for days to come because it was that good. They become the measuring stick you use when having conversations with other people, but no one quite measures up.

These people often possess the following seven characteristics that help make their conversations memorable:

- Every compliment they give means something and comes from their heart. They will never compliment people if they don't mean it.
- Their eye contact is on point. It's never too much, and it's always enough.
- They contribute more than just their time to the conversation. They always add value to it, no matter what the topic at hand is.
- They pay attention and listen with intent.
- They make a point to remember the name of the person they are speaking to and use it during the conversation.
- They always keep the conversation going, whether it's asking open questions or sharing their latest series obsession.
- They get excited about the information shared with them, and they show enthusiasm when conversing.

Do you wish to be that person? We all do! The best place to start with becoming that person is by understanding the basics of conversation.

THE FLOW OF CONVERSATION

A great conversationalist knows when to talk, when to listen, and when to let the silence linger. Overall, there are five stages to every conversation. Understanding the stages and when it should happen is important in becoming a better conversationalist.

Initiation

This stage is the very beginning of the conversation where effort is already required. We can't just jump into the nitty gritty and expect a favorable demeanor from the other person. The initiation phase normally involves some small talk to feel comfortable and "break the ice" so to speak.

Nonverbal communication also plays a role here. The more open and friendly we are when approaching the person to initiate the conversation, the more receptive they will be during the conversation.

Preview

This is where we state the intention of the discussion and give them a little preview of what they can expect during the conversation. Refer back to Chapter 1 where intentions were discussed in detail.

If it's just a friendly conversation, there is no reason to try and fluff it up. We can be direct and honest about what we would like to discuss. When the topic is a little more sensitive, a direct approach might instill panic and cause the other person to shut down.

Business

Here is where we get down to business. During this stage, we can outline what we want to discuss during the conversation, almost like covering an agenda when starting a meeting.

It might not always be as formal as that, but if you really pay attention to even casual conversations, there are generally a list of topics covered that tie back to the main point of the conversation.

Feedback

This stage is as important as all the others. This is where we make sure that we're on the same page. If there are any points that need clarifying, here is where you need to discuss it.

In some situations, we can be as direct as asking whether everyone is on the same page.

Closing

This is where the conversation ends and both parties move on to their next order of business, if applicable. This can only occur if both parties are on the same page during the feedback stage, or else a few points may need to be revisited.

ELEMENTS OF CONVERSATION

Various elements may play a role in a conversation. By knowing about and understanding the different elements, we are better able to control the conversation and ensure that both parties benefit from it.

Some or all of the following elements may be present:

- **Asking**: Gaining more information. It is also used to fully engage in the conversation and dive deeper into what is provided.
- **Asserting**: Putting forward information that is true and accurate.
- **Attacking**: Being destructive and disregarding the other person's thoughts and/or ideas.
- **Avoiding**: Being unwilling to accept the other person's argument.
- **Building**: Providing additional information to ideas already shared to build a better understanding.
- **Challenging**: Providing your new thoughts or ideas to change or question what was already put forward.
- **Checking**: Making sure the other person understands what has been conveyed.
- **Defending**: Stopping the other person from attacking by restating your ideas and why they're valid.
- **Informing**: The opposite of asking in which you are the one providing additional information.

- **Proposing**: Putting forward an idea or argument for the other person to consider.
- **Summarizing**: Providing a brief summary of your understanding of the information provided.
- **Supporting**: Making sure the other person knows that you are there for them.

THE SEVEN CS OF CREATIVE CONVERSATION

According to Fred Dust (2020), there are seven main elements to creative conversation. By engaging in creative conversation, people are more likely to lean in and participate and be willing to reconnect at a later stage. It allows all parties involved to challenge their own thinking and explore new ideas.

Change

There is a point in every conversation where it needs to move forward, and what they are focused on needs to change. For instance, in a brainstorming session, there must be a point where everyone moves on from the problem and starts thinking of creative ways to solve and implement ideas.

Clarity

To have creative and meaningful conversations, it's important that clarity exists in the conversation. Jargon and complex words can easily get lost in conversation and confuse the other person. They might have a different understanding of a specific word than we do, which could lead to a complete misunderstanding. Clearing up jargon and complex words upfront can be helpful, or it can just keep the conversation simple and clear.

Commitment

In normal conversations, we like to get our point across and make sure that everyone else conforms to what we're saying. When it comes to creative conversations, we need to be more open-minded and allow the conversation the freedom to explore new areas and ideas. We need to commit to the people we are communicating with and the conversation itself, not to a specific idea.

Constraints

When rules for a conversation are set by one person and not agreed upon by everyone, it could hinder creativity and effective communication. However, rules are still important to any interaction as it helps to keep everyone in line and focused on the aim of the discussion. Setting these rules or constraints together can make a difference to how the other person or people respond to them.

Context

The setting in which we have certain conversations influence the outcome of it. The environment really sets the scene for the conversation and determines the context in which the discussion will be perceived. For instance, a professional conversation around budget will most likely take place in a boardroom and not the corner coffee shop.

When the environment is not fit for purpose, we can always move a few items around and add or remove the ones that will help set the scene.

Creative Listening

We've already established that active listening doesn't come naturally, and neither does listening in general. Creative listening is not much different in that sense. So, what makes creative listening different to other types of listening?

With creative listening, we help the other person convey their message better. We allow them to challenge their own perspectives and create new ideas. It also helps us as the listener to appreciate our own reactions. Listening creatively opens up more possibilities to where the conversation might go.

Creation

It's no use coming up with great and creative ideas but never letting them come to life. During this stage, the conversation ends, and everyone moves into creation mode.

RULES OF CONVERSATION

There are a few rules that we can follow during any conversation to ensure that it's a meaningful and impactful one. Below are 11 rules I have put together to help.

Avoid Interrupting the Other Person

This is one of the golden rules of conversation, which is why it has been mentioned more than once. Never interrupt someone while they're speaking. They might lose their train of thought or decide to disengage because it seems like you're not interested in what they have to say.

Don't Dwell On Unnecessary Details

This refers to anything that may be irrelevant to the conversation or won't make a difference in the outcome. The other person might lose interest in the conversation if you start talking to them about the time your uncle took you fishing, when the actual conversation was about the books you've recently read.

Be Focused on the Conversation

Don't try to multitask while you're having a conversation. Avoiding your phone and the distractions around you is a great way to let the other person know you value their time. If you're waiting for an important text or phone call, let the person know beforehand so they don't think you're rude when you don't respond or take the call.

Give Them Airtime Too

Try not to hog the conversation too much. Ideally, a conversation should be 50/50, with you talking half the time and the other person getting the other half.

Letting them talk will make them feel heard and sharing your own thoughts and ideas might challenge their thinking and get them excited to engage again.

Just Be Yourself

People appreciate those who can be themselves, regardless of the circumstances. It's important to get your viewpoints across and be true to who you are.

Keep Things Positive

It's always good practice to try and keep conversations positive and upbeat and avoid any negative conversations. Sometimes, especially in the workplace, it might be difficult if you need to address someone's attitude or behavior.

When you're just engaging in casual conversation, steer away from any topics that may cause animosity, such as religion and politics. If you know something is going to upset you, avoid the conversation if you can.

Respect the Other Person's Views

We all have different views on the same thing, which is what makes us unique. If we were all the same, there would be no way for anyone to stand out above the rest. There would be no use for conversation since we all agree and have the same perception. Life would be pretty boring.

So, respect the other person's views and don't try to degrade them or judge them in any way. They have a right to their own opinion.

Show Genuine Interest

It's easy to see when someone is not really interested in something we're saying. When that happens, we're less likely to engage in conversation again, regardless of whether it's on the same topic or a different one.

While in conversation, show genuine interest in what the other person is saying and ask them questions.

Throw in Some Purposeful Questions

Getting to know the other person is an important part of not only a conversation, but also building a relationship. Make them think a little harder and go beyond surface-level discussions by asking them purposeful questions, like what drives them in life or what keeps them up at night.

Don't Bombard Them With Questions

While you should definitely ask a few thought-provoking and open-ended questions, make sure that a question is fully answered and understood before you ask the next one.

CHAPTER 5 SUMMARY

- Every conversation has a natural flow to it. There is the initiation, preview, business, feedback, and closing.
- During the flow of the conversation, various elements may play a role. The elements in the conversation will depend on what it is about and what the intent of the conversation is.
- Creative conversations take a little more effort than normal ones and consist of change, clarity, commitment, constraints, context, creative listening, and creation.

The next chapter talks about the skills of holding a conversation and making it interesting.

CONFIDENCE, CHARISMA, CHARACTER

S o, you managed to initiate a conversation with someone, but now what? How do you keep the conversation flowing naturally without looking like you're trying too hard, or referring back to cue cards for discussion points? Knowing when to end the conversation is just as important as initiating it and keeping it going.

If you want to be the person everyone is thrilled to talk to, you need to learn how to have dazzling, blow-your-socks-off, remember-it-until-you're-85 kind of conversations. This is where your confidence, charisma, and character come into play.

Think about the value that Robert Downey Jr. adds to the Marvel movies in his role as Iron Man. Honestly, his charm, charisma, and confidence are evident in every scene. He really brings the character to life and gives us so much more to appreciate.

The points we cover in this chapter will guide you to make an impact on others just by being in their presence, just like Robert Downey Jr.

That sounds good, doesn't it? Let's jump right into the "how-to" behind it.

SET AN INTENTION

We have already discussed this in detail in Chapter 1. Not having a game plan for a conversation is similar to driving somewhere but not knowing how to get there.

Setting an intention is not just relevant to professional conversations. You can set an overall intention for any social event or even a casual conversation, though there is no need to let the other person know what your intention is.

If you're getting ready for an event where there will be people to network with, there are a few questions you can ask yourself to set your intention. Questions involving the who, what, why, and when of the event:

- Who is hosting, and who will be there?
- What is the event about? What type of people might you encounter? What is the schedule like?
- Why did you decide to go?

- When is the event being held?

Answering these questions might help you come up with a simple one-liner to explain your intention. Something like, "I want to expand my client base" or "I need a night out" is perfect.

MAKE A GOOD FIRST IMPRESSION

We all know how important this is yet, we sometimes manage to get it wrong.

We don't create the first impression when we start talking to someone. The first impression is made the moment we see the person, or they see us, with or without the other person's knowledge. This is why it's important to always be cognizant of our body language and the way others perceive us.

Have you ever seen someone walk into a room and immediately they have everyone's attention? They radiate confidence and seem so approachable. We might admire them because they have an uncanny ability to put people at ease and draw others in.

The way we enter a room plays a big role in the kind of conversations we might have. There are a few things we can do to ensure we seem just as approachable as the person described above when we walk into the room.

- Your hands should always be visible and relaxed. Clenched fists or fidgeting is a big no-no.
- You can make yourself look taller, confident, and relaxed by rolling your shoulders down and back slightly.
- As soon as you spot someone that you know or want to talk to, let a smile spread across your face. It doesn't matter whether they're looking at you or not, someone else might be, and a smile makes you seem friendly and approachable.
- When approaching someone to initiate a conversation, make eye contact and smile before you greet them. Radiating with confidence and showing that we are open to the conversation will make a huge difference.

The first time we see someone, our brains try to place them in a friend or foe category. Following the above tips will ensure that you fall within the friend category every time, improving the probability and quality of the conversations exponentially.

ASK A NUMBERS QUESTION

Jerry Seinfeld shares this tip in a video, and it guarantees an answer every time (Science of People, 2021). The question does not include numbers, but the answer will. These questions help people engage easily and instantly make them feel comfortable.

Asking a numbers-based question is a great small-talk technique to keep the conversation going. It allows us to find out more about the person, and all we need to do is wait patiently for them to say something we can use as a starting point for the conversation. We can use this technique in just about any setting.

Why is this so powerful? Here's the science behind it.

Regardless of who we are and how comfortable we are with the person we're talking to, the first few seconds of a conversation can be quite daunting. Our adrenaline is high in anticipation of the conversation, and if someone asks us a numbers question, it gives us time to calm down and feel comfortable with the interaction. The question and answer are very specific and not something we need to think about. So, when someone asks us, "What did you do this weekend?" or "What are your hopes and dreams for the future?" early in a conversation, this pushes our adrenaline even higher because we don't have a ready answer.

So, help others feel comfortable too! Start off with one (or a few) numbers questions to get the conversation flowing.

Some examples of numbers-based questions include:

- How long was your trip to get here?
- When did you move to LA?

- When are you going on vacation? How long are you going for?
- How many churros have you had?

The type of question will completely depend on the setting. Reading the room is very important when asking these questions and they're absolute gold!

HAVE A FEW CONVERSATION STARTERS IN YOUR BACK POCKET

Not literally. But it's good to have a few conversation starters that you're comfortable with to fall back on if all else fails.

I know how terrifying it can be to try to start a conversation with someone but not know how to initiate it, or worse, not know who to talk to! Sometimes we default to people we already know just because we won't need a conversation starter since the relationship is already there.

Adding to your social circle is always a good idea, and by having a few conversation starters in the back of your mind, you'll be able to talk to anyone at a party or event! Let's have a look at some of the most common and effective conversation starters.

- This first one is a no-brainer, and everyone knows it. It's the old "Hey, how are you?" that gets used so often. Although it is a great conversation starter, people have gotten into the habit of responding with a very short and surface-level answer, which may not lead to much of a conversation.

- You can always take inspiration from the environment by asking the other person how they're liking the food, or what they think of the venue. It's the equivalent of bringing up the weather. It really works!

- When you are at an event where you don't know a lot of people, asking them what they do for a living is a good conversation starter. Not only have you initiated a conversation with someone you don't know, but you also get to know about what they do, which is great when you're trying to expand your network.

- You can also strike up a conversation based on a mutual interest. For instance, if you see them take a flier on extreme sports, you can ask them what they've done and what is still on their bucket list.

- If all else fails, you can talk about the weather. Depending on the type of person you're talking to, they may make a joke about you bringing up the weather, which will instantly break the ice.

Pay attention to the conversation openers other people use to get a conversation flowing and add it to your mental library. You can never have too many!

BE CURIOUS!

People often use the saying that "curiosity killed the cat." The truth is that a healthy amount of curiosity to know more about the person you are talking to helps the conversation flow naturally. The more you know about someone, the easier it will be to find other things to talk about.

In saying that, remember that not every person will be as comfortable to share extremely personal details about themselves. If you haven't formed a deep connection with someone yet, asking about their childhood traumas may not go well.

When meeting someone new, we need to be cognizant of the fact that they might be a private person and keep our curiosity and questions on surface-level subjects until we have established a definite connection. The person might start offering up personal information as the connection grows, which we can use to ask more questions.

While we're on the topic, it's also important for us to share with the other person. We can't expect them to give us personal details about their lives if we're not willing to do the same.

USE BOOKMARKING

We bookmark something when we want to return to a specific page or chapter because it was significant to us, or to continue where we left off. The same can be done during conversations. It's a little tricky sometimes but worth the effort.

When bookmarking something in a conversation, we basically put emphasis on something specific to create or develop a deeper connection with the other person. We add bookmarks to a conversation so that it's easier and more natural for us to follow up or pick up where we left off the last time.

Here are some ways to use bookmarking to your advantage during conversations.

- **The "see you there" bookmark**: We can use this bookmark when someone we are talking to mentions they are going to the same event as us. For example, maybe there is a course on a subject that you're really interested in and have signed up for, and the person you are talking to mentions that they will be taking the same course. You can bookmark the occasion by saying something along the lines of, "I'll also be there. We should grab a bite after one of the classes," and then follow up with them later on.
- **Having something in common and pointing it out**: This is a great way to make others feel more connected to us, even if it's something silly, like both being the middle child. It creates a different connection and lets us relate to someone on a

different level, which we can use to bookmark a follow-up. For instance, let's use the middle child example. When the other person says they are also the middle child, we can follow up with, "I feel like you're the only person that will understand my struggles! We should get together and compare notes." You can connect with them on social media and send them memes or TikToks about being a middle child, which is something you will both enjoy.

- **Sharing an inside joke**: This one is a little more difficult to come across, but absolutely amazing when it happens. This is where we share a funny moment with someone else, which you can bookmark and bring up in a different, but relevant, scenario. It's okay to milk the joke a little bit. It helps us to develop a deeper bond with the other person.

LOOK FOR SPARKS

Initiating a conversation is already difficult without having to worry about how to keep it going. A great way to make sure a conversation flows, and the person feels excited to talk to you is to look for sparks within the conversation and focus on those. A spark is created when dopamine levels increase in our brains, and we feel excited about something.

Bringing up a topic the person is passionate about or looking forward to can create a spark and keep things fun and interesting. Here are some ideas to play around with:

- What's on the itinerary for your upcoming trip?
- Do you have any exciting plans for the weekend?
- Have you been to any new restaurants lately?
- What exciting project are you working on at the moment?
- I saw you got a new puppy. Tell me about them.

If you notice a change in their level of excitement, use that to keep the conversation going.

IT'S ALL IN THE EYEBROWS

The eyebrows are a subtle body-language giveaway, but if you know to look for it, you'll never miss it again. You also can't stop yourself from doing it during a conversation.

When we hear or see something interesting, one or both eyebrows tend to raise as soon as we do. It can be very subtle or very noticeable, but it will always happen. We can use these eyebrow raises as sparks in the conversation. If we notice that the person we're talking to raises their eyebrow when we say something, we can make a mental note and come back to that topic.

For instance, if we're telling someone about our vacation and they raise their eyebrow when we mention some sports car we saw, we can finish our story and start a new conversation about sports cars. We don't need to have a lot of knowledge on the topic because the other person will probably do most of the talking.

BODY LANGUAGE SPEAKS LOUDER THAN WORDS

We need to make sure that the other person knows we are really happy to be there talking with them, regardless of what the topic is. Maintaining an open body language, smiling, and nodding while they're speaking to you are ways to showcase this and encourage them to continue.

Face your body towards them and make eye contact as discussed in Chapter 3.

BE A STORYTELLER

Have you ever listened to someone tell a story and it felt like you were there? You smell the grass under their feet, feel the cool air on your skin, and hear the dogs bark in the distance. You get excited for the highs, and your mood drops slightly with the lows, hoping it gets better.

Using that kind of engagement, we can tell stories to get a point across or explain why we prefer a specific type of chocolate. Using a captivating story makes sure that the people around us pay attention and remember what we said long after the conversation has ended.

Everybody loves hearing about personal experiences. It helps us to live ourselves into the moment and understand the other person better because every experience forms a part of us.

A word of caution to the wise: We should listen more than we talk. Although using a story in a conversation to grab their attention is great, we shouldn't hog all the airtime. Allow the other person to share some stories too.

THE ENDING

A conversation can be amazing, but if you want to leave a lasting impression, you need to know how to end it. One of the most memorable ways to end a discussion is using one of the bookmarks created earlier in the conversation. Here are some examples based on the bookmarks discussed earlier:

- **See you there**: "I'm really looking forward to seeing you at that course next month. I'll text or email you."
- **Having something in common**: "It was great to meet someone that can relate to my struggles as a middle child. Definitely made my night!"
- **Inside joke**: "I had so much fun laughing with you. I'll definitely xyz in the future." (Replace xyz with the inside joke.)

A FINAL NOTE

We should never try to outdo the other person. How many times have you been in a conversation where it doesn't matter what you say because the other person has something even better (or worse) to say so they can win the conversation. If you say that you had a flat tire coming to work this morning, they will say they had two flat tires and no one to help them. If you say that you're going on leave for two weeks, their leave will be for three weeks, and they're going somewhere amazing. It's a really unattractive trait to have and something we should avoid. We might think we're simply trying to relate to the other person, but they might not see it the same way.

Let them have their moment without trying to outdo them. There is a big difference between trying to relate and trying to outdo.

It might be quite difficult to implement any of these if your mindset is in the wrong place. Many of us might struggle with self-sabotage and a closed mindset due to our past conversational experiences. If that sounds like you, don't forget to check out my other book that is available on Amazon: *Help Me, I'm Stuck.* In that book, I share six techniques to help you get unstuck and change your mindset for the better! I really think you'll enjoy it.

CHAPTER 6 SUMMARY

- There are certain guidelines you can use to excel as a conversationalist and have meaningful engagements that people will remember for a long time.
- People create a first impression of us long before we even know they noticed us. We should always carry ourselves with confidence, assuming someone is watching all of the time.
- Numbers-based questions are best when the anxiety levels are running high and we're unsure what to talk about.
- There is nothing wrong with doing some research beforehand and having a few topics in mind to raise at a particular event or with a specific person.
- Bookmarking is a great way to make a lasting impression and have something to remind the other person of the conversation.
- Paying attention to body language goes a long way to knowing whether someone is interested in a particular topic or not.

The next chapter talks about small talk and aims to make you an expert at it.

SMALL TALK GURU

S mall talk can be the worst. Before I started this journey, it was one of the things that made me the most nervous about a conversation, yet most of them have some form of small talk involved before you get into it. In most instances, my small talk attempts used to go something like this:

- Person 1: "So, what do you do for a living?"
- Person 2: "I'm a teacher for third graders."
- Person 1: "That's cool." (No effort to keep the conversation going.)
- Person 2: "Yeah, what do you do?"
- Person 1: "I just lost my job."
- Person 2: "Oh, sorry to hear that."

What an awkward conversation, right! There were so many opportunities for the conversation to go in a different direction, but we both just made it super awkward.

Let's cover some of the basics of small talk. We'll look at this conversation again at the end of the chapter and see whether we can spruce it up a little based on our newly found knowledge.

WHAT IS SMALL TALK?

Small talk is the (almost always awkward) bit of conversation that we have with someone we barely know. It's the surface-level comments and questions that help us fill silences and get to know the other person better if that is the goal. A small-talk topic is generally used as a conversation starter when talking to strangers or acquaintances. It helps us to build rapport with others.

Making small talk can be more difficult for some people than others. It seems to come naturally to some, while the rest of us are left sweating whenever we need to stroke up a conversation with small talk. I'm convinced that we've all had disastrous small-talk conversations, which can also taint our confidence for the future.

By learning the basics of small talk, we can build confidence to better enable us to connect with others. It might seem very superficial, but some of the most meaningful conversations and relationships start with a bit of small talk. The key is to know where to steer the discussion.

There are a few set small-talk topics that are foolproof that you can always turn to, but without an understanding of how to keep the conversation going without hitting a brick wall, it can still take a wrong turn within seconds. Let's look at the who, what, where, when, and why of small talk.

THE FUNDAMENTALS OF SMALL TALK

Who

Most people use small talk in their different relationships, but it is used most commonly among those who are still strangers or mere acquaintances. Colleagues who don't know each other well may also use small talk when they pass each other in the hallway just to not seem rude.

Some jobs may also require people to use small talk, such as retail workers, salespeople, restaurant employees, customer service workers, receptionists, bartenders, and hairdressers. It helps them to boost their sales.

What

Overall, there are a few acceptable small-talk topics that are used more often than others. Here is a list of the most popular small-talk topics among strangers. We tend to use these as conversation starters with our families on occasion as well.

- **The weather**: The most controversial yet most-used topic is the weather. It's bound to break the ice, and everyone has an opinion on it. It's easy to get a conversation started on just the weather.
- **Entertainment news**: This might not be everyone's cup of tea but discussing celebrities and their whereabouts is a passion for some.
- **Current events**: This is another hot topic for small talk if you keep up with current events. If you don't, it's best you start. Others may choose to use this as a conversation starter, and if we don't know enough about what's happening, the conversation might not flow easily. If you're the one initiating the discussion on current events, make sure you stay away from any controversial news, such as legal battles and political affairs.
- **Sports**: This is a favorite among many, especially if the team you or they support are playing soon. Discussing a recent game or one that's coming up is an easy way to get the conversation going.
- **Having something in common**: If you can't find anything specific to chat about, and none of the above strike your fancy, talking about something you have in common with the other person is a good topic to use. For instance, discussing the new layout of the office with your colleagues.

There are also some taboo topics when it comes to small talk, especially with people you don't know that well. These include:

- **Overly personal topics**: This includes personal details, such as the situation at home, salaries, and their finances.
- **Gossip**: The conversation should definitely not include any negative gossip about another person. Putting someone else in a bad light in their absence can raise questions about your character.
- **Body image**: Although talking about someone else's fashion sense and their hair color is okay, it is never acceptable to talk about or comment on their body.
- **Politics**: Avoid this at all costs.

Where

The short answer to this question is anywhere and everywhere! But there are a few places where small talk would occur more often than others, such as:

- **Waiting for something**: For example, waiting at a wedding while the couple is taking photos, waiting for an event or class to start, waiting for the bus, waiting in line to get coffee, etc.
- **At a party or social event**: Small talk is quite common among individuals who don't know each other very well.

When

Small talk normally occurs in the very beginning of a conversation when we speak to the person for the first time that day or at an event. Once the small talk is out of the way, there is no need to make small talk again when we see them later on.

It's important to never interrupt an existing conversation to make small talk. This also extends to when someone is in a virtual meeting, listening to music on their headphones, or reading a book. Always wait for the other person to acknowledge you before initiating conversation. Once eye contact has been made and smiles exchanged, small talk can start.

Why

The main reasons we make small talk with others is to avoid or break uncomfortable silences or to have something to do, which is why we often make small talk when we are waiting for something with someone else.

Another reason why we make small talk is simply to be polite, especially when they start talking to you first.

MAKING SMALL TALK

The aim is not just to make small talk and hope for the best. Our intention is to make small talk meaningful and possibly add value to the other person in some way. This will separate us from the rest who are just making small talk for the sake of it. Most might feel like small talk is a waste of time for that exact reason, which is why we should try to make it different.

A great way to get into the right mindset here is to stop focusing on the fact that it's small talk and that we barely know the other person, and approach it with an inquisitive mind. If we put ourselves out there to learn something from the other person, the chances of success will be much higher.

Here are some tips for making more meaningful small talk.

Be Curious

This is a point I can't stress enough. The more curious we are, the more we will know about the other person, and the more the other person will feel valued and heard. Don't let your curiosity get the best of you and ask them about their divorce within the first five minutes; be interested in what they're saying and try to find new conversation starters within the small talk.

Avoid What You Are Passionate About

Don't talk about what you are most passionate about unless the other person brings up the topic. When we talk about our favorite things, we tend to do most of the talking and very little listening. We can't help it because we're just so passionate about it. This is why it's best to avoid it.

Understand the Why

Try to understand the "why" behind it. We tend to lean more toward asking (and explaining) the "what" of a certain situation that we miss an opportunity to connect with the other person, even with small talk. When they share something, we can challenge their thinking and expand our knowledge by trying to understand the "why."

For example, if we ask someone what they do for a living, it might be a very short and abrupt answer, forcing us to carry the conversation by asking another question. But if we ask why they chose a specific profession, they are more likely to offer additional information, allowing the conversation to flow more naturally.

Ask for Advice

Lean on the other person for advice. This may not work if we don't know the person very well, but we can use this on acquaintances or work colleagues if we seek to build a better connection with them. When someone is giving advice based on their experiences, it activates the same area in the brain when they're eating really good food or having a good time (The Editors of Goop, 2016). By asking someone's advice on a particular matter, we're making them feel good about themselves, which will translate into them wanting to spend more time talking to us.

Offer Additional Information

We should always aim to give a bit of extra information when asked something during small talk. Not everyone has been privy to the contents of this book, and they may be struggling to make small talk. Help them out by giving extra information even if they didn't ask for it. For example, if someone asks what you did last weekend, you can tell them you went on a hiking trip with the kids. Now they already know that you enjoy hiking and have kids, which gives them something to work with as well.

Body Language

Our body language is important too, even during small talk. Using our body language to show interest in what they're saying can move small talk to a meaningful conversation in no time.

CONVERSATION THREADING

If the small-talk tips shared above are not really your thing, there is a little technique called conversation threading that might just do the trick. It's a skill that needs some practice but is well worth the effort.

Let's use the example at the beginning of this chapter to demonstrate conversation threading and how it could have turned out differently.

The conversation will start off the same.

- Person 1: "So, what do you do for a living?"
- Person 2: "I'm a teacher for third graders."

Person 1 now has an opportunity to turn this around. Instead of replying with a deadened answer, they can use what person 2 said as inspiration to come up with another question.

- Person 1: "That's very interesting! How does it feel to be the favorite person to so many young minds?"
- Person 2: "It's such a rewarding job. I absolutely love it. Those kids have become like my own, and for half the day, I get to have them all to myself."
- Person 1: "I bet it's amazing. Tell me about your favorite student? I know you're not supposed to have one, but..."

See how different that conversation went? Both people are now comfortable in the conversation, and it definitely won't end with the next reply.

What Is It?

In short, conversation threading is looking out for threads in a conversation that you can pull on to make the conversation last longer. We need to always be vigilant of what the other person is saying so that we can pick up on these threads and pull on them when we need to. Even though the conversation started with what person 2 does for a living, they are now making jokes and talking about person 2's favorite student. The dialogue already progressed in just two replies.

How to Do It

What is a thread, and how do you pull it? Well, a thread can be anything the person mentions that might be a topic of interest. For instance, if you ask what they like to do for fun and they reply that they enjoy sipping on wine while reading, you have threads that you can pull.

The first is wine. They're wine drinkers, and you can ask them an open-ended question related to that. For example, what kind of wine they enjoy or whether they have ever been to a wine farm and ask them about that experience.

The second thread is reading. They like books. You can ask them about their favorite book, which one they would recommend to anyone and why, whether they're reading anything good at the moment, etc.

Once the person responds to the question, there might be more threads you could use to keep the conversation going. At the same time, you don't always have to use existing information. You can also start a whole new thread if you want to.

Here's a short action plan for creating conversational threads. Remember, it's a process and it might take a while to learn the skill. You can learn it in steps.

- Practice how to listen actively to what other people are saying.
- Learn to pick up on any conversational threads that are worth exploring while listening.
- Use the threads you identified to ask an open-ended question that will get them talking. Just a yes or no question is not a good idea, unless it's part of the bigger picture. For instance, you might need to confirm whether they will be taking some time off for summer vacation before asking what their plans are.

Examples of Conversation Threading

Let's look at a few more examples of conversation threading. We will refer to person 1 simply as P1 and person 2 as P2.

Example 1

- P1: "What did you do this weekend?"
- P2: "I went to the cinema with my sister." (P1 has given two threads: cinema and sister.)
- P1: "I love going to the cinema! What did you see?"
- P2: "We saw the new Aquaman film. I haven't been there in so long and had a really great time."

- P1: "I bet. I've been meaning to see that film. Would you say it's one of your favorite DC films?"

P2 could have easily started a new thread asking about P1's siblings, since they mentioned a sister. If the conversation seems to come to an end, they can always bring it up later (i.e., "You mentioned your sister. I don't have any siblings. How was it growing up with an older/younger sister?").

Example 2

- P1: "Crazy weather we're having today, huh?"
- P2: "Yeah, definitely. I miss the sunshine. The rain makes me miserable."
- P1: "Yeah, I can definitely relate. What do you like to do when the sun shines?"

Here, P1 has taken a negative response and turned the conversation positive again by asking something P2 enjoys.

- P2: "I love going to the beach and just soaking up the sun. It reminds me of summer vacations with my family when I was little."
- P1: "That sounds amazing! Where was your favorite place to go?"

Suddenly the conversation is about their childhood and happy memories. P1 already knows a lot more about P2 just by bringing up the weather.

P1 can continue this thread, but P2 also offered their family as an additional thread that can be explored further.

Example 3

- P1: "Are you looking forward to the weekend?"
- P2: "Not really. I don't have much planned except for work."
- P1: "What work do you do?"
- P2: "I'm a nurse at xyz hospital."
- P1: "Wow, that's amazing. It must be such a rewarding job to help so many people on a daily basis."
- P2: "Yeah, the hours are long. But I can't imagine myself doing anything else."
- P1: "What made you get into that profession?"

Although P2 has expressed that they are not looking forward to working this weekend, P1 has tapped into the reason P2 got into the field in the first place, which is sure to lift their mood.

The goal is to keep the conversation going; however, we want the person to enjoy their conversations with us. If we focus on the negative and build a thread on that, they will associate the conversation negatively and not feel too excited to speak to us again.

CONVERSATION THREADING EXERCISE

Let's do a fun little exercise on conversation threading! After all, practice makes perfect.

I have included some examples below where someone has offered information that can be used for conversation threading. What you need to do is find three different directions the conversations can go based on the information offered.

- I've been playing the piano since I was a little girl. My dad used to teach me a new song every weekend at my grandmother's house.

- We went to London for a family vacation and got to see all the great landmarks. Although I love hiking, we decided to use the bus tours instead.

- I managed to reconnect with a friend from college, and we had the best time at that new coffee shop down the road.

CHAPTER 7 SUMMARY

- Most of us struggle with small talk, and just the mention of it could elicit an anxiety response.
- With specific techniques and a dash of confidence, we can all be masters at small talk.
- When small talk fails us, something that is sure to avoid awkward silences and lead to meaningful interactions is conversation threading.
- With conversation threading, we should always look for new information that has been presented and ask another open-ended question to keep the conversation going.

The next chapter talks about being a natural when it comes to conversations, even when you're mentally breaking down the various aspects of each sentence and taking mental notes of topics to draw the conversation back.

BEING A NATURAL

I t's easy to still be bad at conversations even though you have all the information and tips you could need. This is because all the preparation might make our conversations sound rehearsed or scripted.

Imagine talking to someone who seems to be referencing cue cards in their pocket every time you look away because they don't know what to talk about. The conversation is all over the place, jumping from one topic to another and never really getting into anything. It feels like they're doing a checkbox exercise to make sure they get through a list of specific, predetermined topics before the conversation even starts.

Have you ever experienced that before? Or maybe your conversations have missed the flow we keep talking about throughout this book. Or you end up going back to a small-talk topic soon after the conversation started.

Here is where we bring it all together. This chapter covers the critical skills needed to be natural at making conversation so that it doesn't feel forced or seem scripted.

IT'S ALL ABOUT PRACTICE!

Practicing with someone else will always be first prize, but there is nothing wrong with practicing on ourselves! We are the best people to practice making conversation with. Despite the idea that talking to ourselves makes us "crazy," it's actually completely normal for us to react to our thoughts in the same way we would to someone talking to us.

For instance, having negative thoughts doesn't mean that we can't talk ourselves out of it. We have the power to change those negative thoughts to more positive ones by encouraging ourselves. That's not much different than having a conversation with ourselves.

I honestly talk to myself all the time. It helps to make sense of my thoughts and feelings. Sometimes, I even practice a conversation with myself before I would have it with someone else. It helps me to prepare for the conversation and hear my thoughts out loud before I share them with someone else. There are even times when talking to myself has helped me solve the problem without needing to raise it with anyone else.

Benefits of Talking to Oneself

There are quite a few benefits to talking to oneself. It improves our emotional control and overall mental performance. Although this practice may have been frowned upon in previous years, it has become quite an accepted way to combine thought with action. Here are some of the benefits we can enjoy when talking to ourselves.

Reinforces Memories

Everyone always thought I was crazy at school when I used to read my study material out loud. At some point, so did I. But it makes sense now. By reading things out loud, we are indirectly talking to ourselves as we can see and hear the words. This helps to commit the information to memory quicker and easier than just reading it.

Improves Cognitive Performance

By talking to ourselves, we stimulate our brain's overall performance. A study noted by Kirkham et al. (2012) reinforces the idea that high cognitive functioning is associated with talking out loud when one is completely focused.

Improves Self-Control

By talking to ourselves, we are able to control our emotional responses to situations that may otherwise upset us.

Talk Ourselves Down

We all get a little upset sometimes and feel like throwing something at the wall. The most effective way to calm down is to talk ourselves down from it. We need to remove ourselves from the situation and then talk to ourselves in the third person, which is shown to produce a calming effect.

We Can Encourage Ourselves

Regardless of where encouragement comes from, it always helps us to keep pushing forward when times get tough. This is why telling ourselves in the mirror how amazing we are is so good for us! It builds more self-confidence and encourages us every step of the way. We can be our own biggest supporters.

It Helps to Organize Thoughts

When it's been a busy day or week, it feels like our brains are so full of clutter. Talking to ourselves can help organize the clutter and help us let go of whatever is not important anymore. For instance, there is no reason to hold on to the fact that the lunch lady gave you a look when you asked her whether the veggies were soft or crunchy. When we don't organize our thoughts, things can quickly get out of hand.

It Makes You a Better Conversationalist

I mean, this is why we're talking about this, right? Practicing conversations with ourselves is one of the best things we can do for our social lives. We can look at all possible responses and play devil's advocate. It helps us to find threads to pull on and keep a conversation going. If we don't want to talk to ourselves, why would anyone else?

Using Positive Self-Talk

Let's take a step back and understand what self-talk is before we get into positive self-talk and how practicing it makes us better conversationalists.

Self-talk is the internal dialogue we have in our minds. Our subconscious influences self-talk and demonstrates our ideas, beliefs, and thoughts. Just reading that should tell you that it can be both positive and negative depending on how we're feeling on the day, and it is also formed by our personality.

Positive self-talk helps us have a better outlook on life and can result in a better quality of life in the long run. It also helps to reduce stress and pain and improve overall health. Other than becoming a better conversationalist, practicing self-talk has a whole range of health benefits!

Using positive self-talk can help us cultivate the self-confidence required to talk to others.

Examples of Positive Self-Talk

Here are some examples of how we can change negative self-talk into a positive one. Don't be too hard on yourself if you don't manage to do it all in one day. Just like everything else, it's a skill that needs to be developed and mastered through practice.

- **Negative**: I failed again. I can't ever get anything right.
- **Positive**: I am so proud of myself for trying. It was really difficult, and I'm glad I took the chance. Next time will be better.
- **Negative**: I don't see this turning out well.
- **Positive**: I will do everything within my power to make sure this works.
- **Negative**: Just thinking about doing this is making my stomach churn. I've never done anything like it before, and I know I'll be bad at it.
- **Positive**: I'm really excited to take on this new challenge. It's the perfect opportunity to grow.
- **Negative**: I've let myself go too much. There is nothing I can do about my weight anymore.
- **Positive**: Admittedly, I'm not at the weight I want to be. But it's not too late to turn things around. I will show up and get into better shape because I care about my health.

Tips for Improving Self-Talk

It can be quite difficult to change the little voice in our heads, but it is possible. Instead of dealing with old Grumpy Gus, let's learn how to have a little peppy cheerleader instead!

Be the Critic

When our inner voice is critical about something we do, we should be the critic for them too. In situations where we are feeling pressured and not in control, our inner voice tends to do some negative self-talk based on the situation. Our job is to pause those thoughts and look for ways to turn it positive before it influences everything we do. For example, when we are talking to someone we like and feel very nervous, we might tell ourselves that the other person is not interested in the conversation and we're blowing it completely, even if it's not true. Recognizing the negative self-talk and turning it positive is sure to turn the whole situation around.

Be a Friend to Yourself

When we talk to our friends, we normally use positive language to encourage and support them. Why do we treat ourselves differently? We should consider and treat ourselves as a friend instead of someone that we're constantly disappointed in. The more we focus on the negative, the more negative we invite into our lives, and the more things will feel like they're going wrong. When we change how we see ourselves, we'll be able to take on anything that comes our way.

Create Some Distance

That sounds so strange, doesn't it? How can we create distance from ourselves? When we make a statement too personal, such as "Why am I struggling with this so much?" it creates even more anxiety and feelings of helplessness. We should distance ourselves from the "I" and replace it with our name, referring to ourselves in the third person. So, using that logic, we would say "Why is (name) struggling with this so much?" Our minds will then start looking for solutions instead of feeling terrible about the fact that we can't get it done.

Rephrase Speech

We are all culprits of putting limitations on ourselves. Sometimes we do it without even realizing it. For example, we tend to use "I can't" quite often, mostly with no malicious intent. Replacing it with "I don't" makes quite the difference. Let's look at some examples:

- "I can't miss my morning run" vs "I don't miss my morning run."
- "I can't make spaghetti bolognaise" vs "I don't make spaghetti bolognaise."

Using "I can't" puts a clear limitation on us, while "I don't" sounds more like a choice we make.

We Choose the Goal

Depending on what we want to achieve with self-talk, we can personalize it with the goal we have in mind. For example, if we need a little encouragement and to build self-confidence, telling ourselves how amazing and capable we are will go a long way. If it's a technique or skill we need to learn, the self-talk we use will be more driven toward the action we should be performing, such as "shoulders down and back" for a better posture.

Practicing positive self-talk is very important because we can't apply something to someone else if we haven't applied it to ourselves. Before we can implement different techniques in conversations with others, we should use what we learn to ourselves first. For example, sincerely commending others should be practiced on ourselves first.

It's okay if it takes some time to learn and master all of the techniques. We shouldn't only look at how much we've done but balance that with how much we have already achieved.

BE SINCERE WITH YOURSELF AND OTHERS

Just like practicing self-talk starts with you, so does sincerity. To truly be sincere with others, we need to be sincere with ourselves. Sincerity allows us to properly lean into a conversation and communicate more effectively with the other person. There are very few things in life as beautiful and magical as a real and sincere connection with someone else.

The problem is that it's very difficult to build this kind of connection. A sincere connection involves listening and sharing, and we all have difficulty building these relationships with people. It requires us to be vulnerable and to let the other person see us without any armor, which comes with the possibility of getting hurt. The only way to really tap into this amazing world of sincerity and unashamed sharing is to be brave enough to chase after these connections and practice sincere (or active) listening at all times.

Sincerity can be built by active listening. This is discussed in detail in Chapter 3, so feel free to refer back to that chapter for a quick recap. To listen actively and effectively means that you listen as if someone's life depends on it. You listen with intent and to understand, not to respond.

For example, if you and your loved ones are caught in a building that was on fire and a fireman was giving you instructions on how to get yourself and everyone else out safely, there is no way you would be thinking about what you'll be cooking for dinner. You will be listening to his instructions with intent and making sure you understand them because people's lives depend on it. We need to make sure that we use this same intent when listening to someone during a conversation.

The example may seem exaggerated, but it gets the point across. If we listen to people in this way, our conversations will be a lot more effective and successful.

Be sincere. Be genuine. They could have chosen anyone else to talk to, and they chose you. Show them they didn't make a mistake.

KEEP THE CONVERSATION GOING NATURALLY

That awkward silence is bound to happen in most conversations when we don't know the other person all that well. It's a terrifying thought and enough to prevent us from talking to someone at all. The good news is that there is a nifty little trick we can use to prevent awkward silence and keep a conversation going, which seems to be effortless.

The 30% Rule

This rule states that 30% of what you say should be new information. This will not only help to keep the conversation interesting but provides a whole bunch of new threads that can be used to keep it going. If the same information is repeated, or it is something the other person already knows from previous conversations, we'll run out of things to say within a matter of minutes.

Adding new information creates endless possibilities for new threads and also helps to build a relationship. The more we know about another person and vice versa, the closer our bond will be.

For example, if the other person says that they had a great night out with you, instead of just replying with "Me too," you could say something like, "Yeah, it was a really great night. I haven't been out in so long. I had a lot of fun dancing with you and getting to know you better. What was your favorite part of the evening?"

This tells them that you haven't had a night out in a while and invites them to tell you what they enjoyed most. They might respond and ask you the same question, keeping the conversation going.

Maybe you're wondering why only around 30% of the information should be new. Surely, the more information we provide, the better? Not exactly. By providing more new information, we might overload them with details or even dominate the conversation.

If there is no way to add any more information to an existing topic, close it off and start a new one. There is no reason you have to make something work if it's not possible.

Remember to use conversation threading as a guideline to help with picking new topics.

You are now prepared to talk to anyone and intrigue them into talking to you even more. You'll be able to carry out these conversations with ease.

Just one more thing: Be confident!

FINAL TIPS ON CONFIDENCE

Being afraid to speak to other people, especially strangers, is completely normal. Most of us go through it. Our brains perceive it as a threat (albeit not a real one, but more of a social threat), which increases our stress hormones and causes us to stumble over our words. There are things we can do to help with confidence during these situations. Some of these have been mentioned and discussed within the book, but we are including them here to show that they have more than one benefit.

- **Acceptance**: It's easier to deal with something when we accept it. So, rather than trying to fight the feeling of anxiety or nervousness, we need to accept it. Remember that everyone deals with nervousness, even confident people.
- **Backtrack**: When things seem to be dying down, going back to previous topics is always a winner.
- **Be vulnerable**: This is not the cue to start crying about the dog you lost when you were five years old, but by being open and sharing things about your life makes a conversation more interesting and captures the other person's attention. The more we share in the conversation, the more they will too.
- **Change the tone**: Using tonal variation can make us come across more confident and charismatic.
- **Focus**: When we focus on the topic at hand, we can come across as more charismatic and authentic. These are important characteristics for confidence. We tend to dwell on things when the other person mentions something that sounds a little out of our comfort zone. In those moments, we should bring ourselves back to the actual topic at hand and not get lost in our own thoughts.

- **Keep eye contact**: When talking or listening, eye contact is quite important; however, when we keep eye contact for too long, it may feel a little intense and awkward. Breaking eye contact is a good idea when we want to take a moment to think about something or gather our thoughts.

- **Let silence linger**: And don't feel like it's your fault at all. The other person is most likely battling with the same thoughts. Knowing this will help take the pressure off and make it easier to come up with something new to talk about. Accept that there will be silences, and don't feel awkward during those. Confident people don't feel awkward in silence; they embrace it.

- **Listen attentively**: This was covered extensively but is an important aspect in being more confident during a conversation. The more we listen, the more information we will have to keep the conversation flowing.

- **Look for nonverbal cues**: Sometimes we're not sure whether someone wants to talk to us or not. Nonverbal cues are great to use as confirmation because it's difficult to change something so innate about ourselves. When talking to someone else, pay attention to where their feet are pointing and where their gaze lingers. If they are interested, their feet will point toward you and their gaze will be on you for most of the conversation; however, when these are pointed away from you, they are probably looking for a reason to leave the conversation.

- **Name it**: Just acknowledging and dealing with the elephant in the room may help. Taking some time to identify and name the nervousness can help take the edge off. This can be done in three steps:

  ○ Identify where in our body the nervousness has settled.
  ○ Accept that it's there and give it a name, like Ben or Sally.
  ○ After accepting it, let it go and continue like nothing happened.

- **Pay attention to posture**: When our posture is confident, we look and feel more confident.
- **Practice makes perfect**: Whether you practice in a mirror, at an event, or with family, practicing making effective conversation goes a long way to improving.
- **Reminder on perceptions**: The way we see ourselves is vastly different from how other people see us, family included. Whether the other person knows us very well or not, they perceive us to be a different person than what we think we are. We know our own struggles and limitations. All they see is who we are in the moments we engage with them.

Use this knowledge to strip away the thoughts that hinder a conversation.

- **Show genuine interest**: Don't just fire off random questions that are unrelated to the topic at hand. Show genuine and sincere interest in what the other person is saying and try to find out more. Make a point to learn something from them.

- **Slow down**: When we get really excited or nervous, we tend to speak a lot faster. This signals to the other person (and our own brains) that we are feeling nervous and reflect a poor self-image, as if we feel like we take up valuable space that someone else can fill. Speaking just a little slower can show confidence and give us some time to think about what we want to say.

- **Speak up**: We should never speak too loud during a conversation, but it should be loud enough that we are heard, and people pay attention.

- **Voice confidence**: If we think about someone who lacks confidence, we are reminded of someone who has a soft voice and is afraid of taking up space. Voice confidence deals with making sure that our voice sounds more confident, whether we feel it or not.

Bonus Tip

A nifty trick I have come to find really works is to convince ourselves that we're not feeling nervous at all. That sounds a little silly because we can feel that we're nervous, right?

Think about what happens to our bodies when we are nervous? Our heart starts racing, we get sweaty palms, our breathing increases, etc. Now, think about what happens to our bodies when we get excited? Our heart starts racing, we get sweaty palms, our breathing increases, etc. The physiological response is the same in both situations. The only difference between anxiety and excitement is the stimulus— whether our brain perceives the stimulus to be something that will excite us or make us anxious.

Using this knowledge, we can convince ourselves that we're actually feeling excited. Instead of saying or thinking, "Wow, I feel so nervous about this," we can rephrase it and say, "I'm really looking forward to this event. I can't believe how excited I am to talk to everyone."

CHAPTER 8 SUMMARY

- Practice makes perfect. Sometimes, we need to practice on ourselves to become better at having conversations.

- We should practice positive self-talk every opportunity we get. Talking to ourselves, especially in a positive manner, holds a myriad of benefits.
- Being sincere and authentic within our relationships, especially the relationship we have with ourselves, is so important to develop meaningful relationships.
- Using the 30% rule with conversation threading can help prevent a conversation from dying down.

CONCLUSION

Setting an intention for any conversation is so important as it adds value to it and the relationship. But what is equally important is to remember that the intentions we set and the impact our actions have are not always aligned. Paying attention to how our actions impact the other person will help us to grow personally and maintain our relationships.

Meaningful relationships are important to develop and maintain as it helps give us a sense of purpose and belonging. We all want to feel like we belong somewhere and developing these authentic connections with other people help to foster those feelings. Really connecting with someone on a different level is so rare and should be cherished and cared for when we get it right.

To develop these relationships and keep the connections alive, we need to learn how to listen. And not just listen to respond but listen to understand. When people feel like they're being listened to, they feel valued and connected to the person doing the listening. Practicing active listening is an important skill to develop and master as it will help improve existing connections and form new ones. The better we are at listening, then the more people will want to talk to us.

In saying all of that, certain barriers still exist within conversations. If we are not aware of our barriers, then we have little to no control over them. Identifying these barriers and putting measures in place to manage them is important for meaningful engagement. Some of these barriers might be more difficult than others to overcome, but none are impossible. For example, if a physical barrier exists, such as hearing loss, alternative methods of communication can be explored.

Every conversation has five parts to it: the initiation, preview, business, feedback, and closing. Knowing what happens during each phase and understanding how they impact the overall conversation are important to understand if we want to be great at communication. We should focus on the seven Cs of creative conversation when engaging with others. These are change, clarity, commitment, constraints, context, creation, and creative listening.

There are specific things that we can do to initiate and hold a conversation while still allowing it to flow naturally. Some of the things we need to consider include setting an intention and making sure we make a good impression. When we've engaged in conversation, we can use the old trick of asking a numbers question, pull out a conversation starter from our back pocket, or choose a small-talk topic to get the conversation going. During the conversation, we need to pay attention to our body language and show genuine interest in the other person. Bookmarking some of the things they say and looking for new sparks to continue the conversation are also important.

Small talk may be daunting, but with a few tricks, we can all become small-talk experts. Understanding the basics of small talk and embracing rather than shying away from these topics may help a great deal when faced with an awkward situation where small talk is required. When all of that fails, conversation threading is an excellent way to get someone else talking and keep them interested in the conversation. Everyone loves talking about themselves, and conversation threading allows us to ask the question, forces us to listen to new information, and gives the other person an opportunity to really share as much as they want to.

All of these tips are great, but it needs glue to hold it all together. We need to make an effort to practice what we learn. We can do that by talking to other people or even talking to ourselves. In fact, it's very healthy to have a conversation with ourselves and practice positive self-talk. This helps to improve self-image and boost self-confidence, which are only two of the benefits associated with talking to ourselves. (No mom, I'm not crazy.)

A sincere and authentic connection with someone else is so rewarding, and in order for us to begin building that connection, we need to start with ourselves and practice active listening. In addition to listening, we also need to be willing to share with the other person. This will allow us to have better conversations that flow naturally.

When conversations don't seem to flow naturally, we can use the 30% rule to fix this. When we're talking to someone, we should offer around 30% of new information every time. If we don't, and we keep recycling known information, the conversation will reach an end a lot faster than it started.

Remember to ooze self-confidence in every situation. I have given you all the tools you need. All you need to do is apply them with confidence. It is the one skill where we can actually fake it until we make it. But remember that even confident people get nervous sometimes, and that's okay too. Acknowledge it, name it, and then move on.

Is this everything you need to know to have amazing conversations with everyone you meet? Not quite, but it's a good starting point. Stay hungry and be open to other ways to increase your ability to speak and connect with others. Always be on the lookout for ways to improve because this is a journey. Observe conversationalist that you admire and be determined to get better every day. And if you haven't done so already, please don't forget to leave a review on Amazon for my book. I love getting feedback from others and knowing that something I've said has made a difference in someone's life.

Until the next time…

P.S. I left a special bonus at the end of this book. Enjoy!

REFERENCES

Admin. (2021, April 23). *Importance of listening skills and its role in effective communication.* IMPOFF. https://impoff.com/importance-of-listening/

Barriers in communication. (n.d.-a). Vedantu. https://www.vedantu.com/commerce/barriers-in-communication

Barriers in communication. (n.d.-b). Toppr. https://www.toppr.com/guides/business-correspondence-and-reporting/communication/barriers-in-communication/

Best, E. (n.d.). *The one rule to keep every conversation going naturally.* Lifehack. https://www.lifehack.org/607243/the-one-rule-to-make-every-conversation-keep-going-naturally

BFC Team. (2017, June 12). *Practicing sincerity through actively listening.* Ben Franklin Circles. https://benfranklincircles.org/sincerity/practicing-sincerity-through-actively-listening

Bongers, A., & Macartney, D. (2019). Conversation. In *Communication at Work.* https://ecampusontario.pressbooks.pub/scientificcommunication/chapter/conversation/

Connolly, M. (2021, August 30). *Manipulation isn't communication.* Conversant. https://www.conversant.com/manipulation-isnt-communication/

Cuncic, A. (2022a, February 14). *Small talk topics.* Verywell Mind. https://www.verywellmind.com/small-talk-topics-3024421

Cuncic, A. (2022b, November 9). *What is active listening?* Verywell Mind. https://www.verywellmind.com/what-is-active-listening-3024343

Dickinson, K. (2022, September 26). *5 reasons talking to yourself is good for you.* Big Think. https://bigthink.com/neuropsych/talking-to-yourself/

DiValentino, A. (2017, September 27). *6 ways you're being manipulative without even knowing it.* Greatist. https://greatist.com/live/ways-you-might-be-manipulative#1

Duczeminski, M. (n.d.). *6 benefits of talking to yourself (no, you're not crazy).* Lifehack. https://www.lifehack.org/299684/6-benefits-talking-yourself-youre-not-crazy

Dust, F. (2020, November 24). *Better conversations: The 7 essential elements of meaningful communication.* Fortune. https://fortune.com/2020/11/24/making-conversation-book-fred-dust-ideo-meaningful-communication/

The Editors of Goop. (2016, April 21). *8 ways to make meaningful small talk.* Goop. https://goop.com/wellness/relationships/8-ways-to-make-meaningful-small-talk/

Edwards, V. V. (n.d.-a). *57 killer conversation starters so you can start a conversation with anyone, anytime.* Science of People. https://www.scienceofpeople.com/conversation-starters-topics/

Edwards, V. V. (n.d.-b). *How to have and hold dazzling conversation with anyone: We review 11 science backed steps.* Science of People. https://www.scienceofpeople.com/have-hold-conversation/

Elements of the conversation. (n.d.). Changing Minds. http://changingminds.org/techniques/conversation/elements/elements.htm

11 reasons to read a bedtime story every night. (n.d.). The School Run. https://www.theschoolrun.com/11-reasons-read-bedtime-story-every-night

Friedman, Milton. (n.d.). *There's nothing that does so much harm as good intentions.* https://www.azquotes.com/quote/647072

Frost, A. (2019, July 24). *The ultimate guide to small talk: Conversation starters, powerful questions, & more.* HubSpot. https://blog.hubspot.com/sales/small-talk-guide

Garner, E. (n.d.). *The seven barriers to communication.* Impact Factory. https://www.impactfactory.com/resources/the-seven-barriers-to-great-communications/

Gehrt, J. (2021, May 27). *Communicating with intention: How to have better conversations.* Communique PR. https://www.communiquepr.com/communicating-with-intention-how-to-have-better-conversations/17275/

Gurteen, D. (n.d.). *The purposes of conversation.* Conversational Leadership. https://conversational-leadership.net/purposes-of-conversation/

Holland, K. (2020, June 26). *Positive self-talk: How talking to yourself is a good thing.* Healthline. https://www.healthline.com/health/positive-self-talk#_noHeaderPrefixedContent

Imafidon, C. (n.d.). *7 reasons why some people's conversations are more memorable.* Lifehack. https://www.lifehack.org/articles/productivity/7-reasons-why-some-peoples-conversations-are-more-memorable.html

The importance of connection through meaningful relationships. (n.d.). Centerstone. https://centerstone.org/our-resources/health-wellness/the-importance-of-connection-through-meaningful-relationships/

The importance of meaningful relationships. (2020, May 15). The Carrington at Lincolnwood. https://www.thecarrington.com/2020/05/15/importance-of-meaningful-relationships/

Jobtraining. (2017, October 16). *Influence conversations setting positive intentions.* https://jobtraining.nl/influence-conversations/

KaraMcD. (2020, January 9). *9 ways to build meaningful relationships that matter.* My Question Life. https://myquestionlife.com/build-meaningful-relationships/

Kirkham, A. J., Breeze, J. M., & Mari-Beffa, P. (2012). The impact of verbal instructions on goal-directed behaviour. *Acta Psychologica, 139*(1), 212–219. https://doi.org/10.1016/j.actpsy.2011.09.016

London, J. (2015, August 25). *Intention in conversation.* LinkedIn. https://www.linkedin.com/pulse/intention-conversation-jeffer-london/

Loopward. (n.d.). *Conversation threading: 4 steps & examples to improve your social skills.* https://loopward.com/improve-conversation-skills-using-conversational-threads-and-sharing-experiences/

MBA TUTS Team. (2018, January 19). *10 rules of a great conversationalist.* MBA TUTS. https://www.mbatuts.com/10-rules-of-a-great-conversationalist/

The Mind Tools Content Team. (n.d.). *Active listening.* MindTools. https://www.mindtools.com/CommSkll/ActiveListening.htm

Mignona, M. (n.d.). *How to build meaningful relationships (and what stops us).* Whole Life Challenge. https://www.wholelifechallenge.com/how-to-build-meaningful-relationships/

Morin, D., & Sander, V. (2021, February 12). *23 tips to be confident in a conversation (with examples).* SocialSelf. https://socialself.com/confident-conversation/

Nash, J. (2020, May 14). *Building healthy relationships with 40 helpful worksheets.* Positive Psychology. https://positivepsychology.com/healthy-relationships-worksheets/

Neal, A. (2020, August 11). *10 basic rules for great conversations.* Sidecar. https://sidecarglobal.com/engage/10-basic-rules-for-great-conversations/

Phimister, F. (2018, April 9). *Why bedtime stories are so important - and how schools can help.* Book Trust. https://www.booktrust.org.uk/news-and-features/features/2018/april/why-bedtime-stories-are-so-important---and-how-schools-can-help/

Psych Central Guest Author. (2015, April 12). *5 tips to improve your self-talk.* Psych Central. https://psychcentral.com/blog/5-tips-to-improve-your-self-talk#1

Reader's Digest Editors. (2022, March 28). *12 golden rules of conversation.* Reader's Digest. https://www.rd.com/article/12-golden-rules-of-conversation/

Riker, R. (n.d.). *How to keep a conversation going - without the stress.* The Social Winner. https://www.thesocialwinner.com/how-to-keep-a-conversation-going-without-the-stress/

Rivers, D. (2012). *Challenge two: Explaining intent & inviting consent.* Communication Skills Resources. https://newconversations.net/communication-skills-workbook/explaining-conversational-intent-inviting-consent/

Roosevelt, F. D. (n.d.). *Franklin D. Roosevelt quotes.* BrainyQuote. https://www.brainyquote.com/quotes/franklin_d_roosevelt_132705

Sam. (2016, September 12). *Eight ways to add value when communicating.* Management 3.0. https://management30.com/blog/power-of-communication/

Science of People. (2020, November 9). *Jerry Seinfeld's conversation hack.* YouTube. https://youtu.be/BExVtFFyEgw

Serai, V. (n.d.). *How to hold a conversation & make people love talking to you.* LovePanky. https://www.lovepanky.com/my-life/relationships/how-to-hold-a-conversation

Shukla, V. (2022, August 22). *What are communication barriers & how to overcome them.* Shine Learning. https://learning.shine.com/talenteconomy/career-help/communication-barriers-and-how-to-overcome-them/

Small talk: Who, what, where, when, why. (n.d.). EnglishCLUB. https://www.englishclub.com/speaking/small-talk_wh.htm

Tarvin, A. (n.d.). *7 qualities of meaningful relationships.* Humor That Works. https://www.humorthatworks.com/learning/7-qualities-of-meaningful-relationships/

Thieving6. (2014, November 4). *Conversational threading: The basics of building conversation with anyone!* Reddit. https://www.reddit.com/r/selfimprove ment/comments/2l8psi/ conversational_threading_the_basics_of_building/

Tung, J., & Milbrand, L. (2022, August 18). *10 tips for making small talk less awkward.* Real Simple. https://www.realsimple.com/work-life/work-life-etiquette/manners/10-big-rules-small-talk

Udemy Editor. (2020, February). *The importance of listening, and ways to improve your own skills.* Udemy Blog. https://blog.udemy.com/importance-of-listening/

Waters, S. (2021, July 14). *Intent versus impact: A formula for better communication.* BetterUp. https://www.betterup.com/blog/intent-vs-impact

White, T. (2021, April 27). *How intent and impact differ and why it matters.* Healthline. https://www.healthline.com/health/intent-vs-impact

Wrench, J. S. (2012). The importance of listening. In *Stand up, speak out: The practice and ethics of public speaking.* Saylor Academy. https://saylordotorg. github.io/text_stand-up-speak-out-the-practice-and-ethics-of-public-speaking/s07-the-importance-of-listening.html

Zaun, M. (2020, February 11). *How to communicate without being manipulative.* LinkedIn. https://www.linkedin.com/pulse/how-communicate-without-being-manipulative-matt-zaun/

ALSO BY VAUGHN CARTER

Vaughn Carter's first book is available now on Amazon.

Read on to sample the introduction...

VAUGHN CARTER

HELP ME, I'M STUCK

Six Proven Methods to Shift Your Mindset
From Self-Sabotage to Self-Improvement

Think Positive
Improve Your Habits
Experience Growth

As I was growing up, I learned many invaluable life lessons. Over the years, some of the most important lessons I learned came from old family friends who grappled with one problem after another.

I watched as those friends struggled with relationships, weight loss, money, and many other things in life. Sometimes I wondered: Why is it so difficult for these strong, talented, and beautiful individuals to get in shape? To choose a good partner? Or to ask for a raise or a promotion?

But I don't wonder anymore. Because now, having become an adult myself, I get it.

Like so many of us, they were stuck.

Each one of them was stuck, limited by their self-belief. By the knowledge that no matter how hard they tried, they couldn't change their circumstances.

No surprise there. Not when you stop to consider that change is rarely easy. In fact, not only is change extremely difficult, for most of us it is downright daunting! Your heart may long for change—to lose those twenty pounds or that mediocre significant other you settled for ten years ago.

But what about when it comes to your mind?

That is another matter entirely. In fact, not only do our minds not believe that change is possible—our minds, in the form of our thought processes, often sabotage us. Don't believe me? Well, just stop and consider:

When was the last time you promised yourself you would lose a few pounds in time for (insert important life event here)?

When did you last swear your limit was two margaritas on a night out—but the tequila tasted so good you ended up drinking four?

When did you last revise a "new and improved" schedule, one that would allow you to accomplish all your goals (this time), plus have free time for yourself (this time)? Until you found that you slipped right back into your old routine within a few days of posting that schedule on your fridge?

When did you promise yourself that you would clean out the spare bedroom (which no one has slept in since 2015) so you could create your home gym (which would be more than enough incentive to begin working out), and which would help you whittle down your middle? Because then you could fit into that red silk dress you bought on clearance at Macy's—you know, the same dress that's been hanging in your closet for five years now, just begging for you to wear it for a night on the town.

If you're like most of us, the mere thought of thinking about the answers to these questions has just added a few wrinkles to your face. Because the truth is that many people sabotage their own ideas, goals, and dreams before they even get started.

Why do we do that? Well, that's another book entirely. In part, it has to do with conditioning. Oftentimes, conditioning that began during your formative years, when you were just a child who had no say over how your life unfolded. Or what people said to you, or did to you.

But this book? This book is here to help you get unstuck, to help you learn how to shift your mindset from self-sabotage to self-improvement. And it contains six proven methods to teach you to do just that.

Because guess what? You can change. We can change. I've seen it happen. And the results are nothing short of amazing.

"We can do it!" isn't just the World War II slogan of Rosie the

Riveter. That iconic phrase was designed to boost morale after women entered the workforce while the menfolk were away fighting. But in the 1980s, this Westinghouse Electric marketing slogan began to gain traction as an empowerment tool for an entirely new generation of women.

The reason Rosie the Riveter was so popular, both then and now, is twofold. First, that poster contains J. Howard Miller's photo of a no-nonsense woman, sleeves rolled up and biceps bulging. Tell me, please, what woman wouldn't die for biceps like that today? I guarantee you that every woman who has a gym membership would.

Second, "Rosie" has come to represent an "I can do it!" attitude for millions of women. In fact, any woman looking for a symbol of confidence will certainly find it in the determined set of Rosie's chin—or the steely glint in her blue eyes.

That wartime poster tells us that no matter the problem, the solution always requires hard work. And yes, change requires effort. Sometimes, monumental effort! I know this. I've squared off against many difficult changes—and come off the victor. It wasn't easy, but it was possible.

I did that by creating a roadmap of sorts. Because it helped me, I know it will do the same for you. My roadmap will help you to avoid the potholes that can bust a tire and send you careening over the edge of a cliff while trying to navigate this highway we call life. Or, if you're already teetering on the edge, my roadmap will help you do a course correction—so you can reach your destination successfully, with both tires and sanity intact.

To understand how this is possible, picture this scenario. Imagine two Pacific islands, identical in every way, but miles apart. On each island is a stranded woman standing alone under the blazing sun, hearing nothing but the lapping waves. And her own thoughts.

Woman A—let's call her Ann—is frightened. Ann worries about being alone. She worries that she can't drink the seawater because it's salty. Nor can she see any food—so how can she possibly survive? Ann also thinks about how painful her sunburn is, how much the sand hurts her feet, and how, without food and shelter, she'll soon end up as supper for the seagulls overhead.

Unable to bear the thought of her fate, Ann curls into a fetal position under one of the palm trees and cries, imagining how distraught her family will be when they learn of her death.

In these scenarios, Woman B—let's call her Beth—is also frightened. But unlike Ann, Beth looks around for any signs of life on the little island and thinks, "surely I'm not alone." Beth knows she can't drink the seawater, but reasons that the plush island vegetation must mean there is potable water somewhere. She just has to find it.

Instead of wondering how she can survive without food or shelter, Beth looks at the fish swimming near the water's edge and starts thinking about how good they'll taste once she figures out how to catch them. Like Ann, Beth is also sunburnt. Too, her feet are blistered—but she can't let a little thing like pain stand in her way. Unwilling to concede defeat, or let her circumstances dictate her fate, Beth refuses to sit down for even a second. Because doing so could cause her to become drowsy. Beth knows that drowsiness could lull her to her own death. And that is a danger Beth cannot risk.

So, which woman are you—Ann? Or Beth?

Perhaps the better question is: which woman do you want to be?

Ann and Beth are in identical circumstances, but who is more helpless? I think we'd all agree that Ann is, because of the power of her thoughts. Ann lets her circumstances control her thoughts. As a result, she is without hope. Lacking all motivation and unable to see the bigger picture, Ann gives up before she ever gets started.

Like Ann, Beth has no money or experience in island living. Still, her thoughts overrule her circumstances. Armed with only one weapon—a different perspective—Beth's chance of survival will beat Anne's by 1,000:1.

Do you feel hopeless? Even if your problem isn't as life-threatening as Ann's, do you see a bit of yourself in her? Are you stuck? Do you have trouble getting motivated?

If so, you're not alone. Don't feel bad; it's not your fault. For the past two decades, experts who study technology have warned us that if we're not careful, we will fall victim to "information overload."[1] This phenomenon can cause our brain to get stuck, not knowing which way to turn next because our mind is trying to focus on too many things.

So, if you identify with Ann, and feel as though you're trapped by your circumstances, this will lead to negative thoughts and feelings. Of course, thoughts and feelings are different, but they work in tandem to generate our actions. And when we're stuck, the results of our actions can turn out to be more detrimental than we realize.

Like Ann, we might curl into a ball and give up, waiting for the waves of life to wash over us. To carry us hither and thither. In fact, we're so paralyzed by our fears that we don't even risk resisting. Nor do we attempt to swim in the opposite direction.

Being stuck is a vicious cycle, leading us nowhere fast.

But take heart, because the six proven methods contained in the following chapters can turn your life around. By following the steps in my book, I promise you that positive change will ensue. Then, in no time, your mindset will shift, moving from a mentality of self-sabotage to one of self-improvement. Allow these steps to help you harness a mindset where you are in the driver's seat. Where you control your thoughts and process your feelings in a healthy and productive way.

Because only then, when you experience positive change, will the world become your oyster.

NOTES

ALSO BY VAUGHN CARTER

1. Watchtower Bible and Tract Society of Pennsylvania. (1998, January 8). *An Overload of Information.* Wol.Jw.Org. Retrieved October 1, 2021, from https://wol.jw.org/en/wol/d/r1/lp-e/101998001